How to Take Great Trips with Your Kids

How to Take Great Trips with Your Kids

Sanford Portnoy
Joan Portnoy

THE HARVARD COMMON PRESS
Boston, Massachusetts

*To Kate, Dave, and Tim,
who continue to make our lives
a wonderful trip*

The Harvard Common Press
535 Albany Street
Boston, Massachusetts 02118

Copyright © 1995 by Sanford Portnoy and Joan Flynn Portnoy

All rights reserved. No part of this publication may be reproduced or transmitted in any form or by any means, electronic or mechanical, including photocopy, recording, or any information storage or retrieval system, without permission in writing from the publisher.

LIBRARY OF CONGRESS CATALOGING-IN-PUBLICATION DATA

Portnoy, Sanford.
   How to take great trips with your kids / by Sanford and Joan Portnoy. — Rev. ed.
     p.   cm.
   Includes index.
   ISBN 1-55832-073-3. — ISBN 1-55832-074-1 (pbk.)
   1. Travel. 2. Family recreation. I. Portnoy, Joan Flynn.
II. Title.
G151.P67   1995
910'.2'02—dc20   95-7411

Cover photograph: E. P. Jones Co.
Cover design by Joyce C. Weston
Text design by Linda Ziedrich

10 9 8 7 6 5 4 3 2 1

CONTENTS

Acknowledgments vi
1 ■ The Pros and Cons of Family Travel   1
2 ■ Different Kids at Different Ages   10
3 ■ Planning Your Trip   18
4 ■ Planes, Trains, Cars, and RVs   43
5 ■ Packing for the Trip   65
6 ■ Managing en Route   72
7 ■ Lodgings—Choosing Them, Enjoying Them   84
8 ■ Family Resorts and Cruises   109
9 ■ Traveling as a Single Parent   115
10 ■ Staying Healthy Away from Home   123
11 ■ Games for Traveling Families   135
12 ■ Family Travel ABCs   153
Appendix   157
Index   167

ACKNOWLEDGMENTS

We would like to express our appreciation to the people who were kind enough to read and critique sections of the manuscript for this book. For the original edition, Richard E. Jones and Thomas W. Becker of Delta Airlines, Richard B. Johnson of Northwest Airlines, Bruce Daigler of Swissair, and the helpful folks at Amtrak provided expertise on transportation; Leo J. Meehan, Jr., of the Public Health Service, and Drs. Victor Tesoriero, Eugenia Marcus, and John Cohen helped with the medical chapter; and Dr. Jaine Darwin reviewed the child development material. For the revised edition, Drs. Eugenia Marcus, Leonard Marcus, and Arthur Kennedy reviewed the medical chapter.

We would also like to thank the travel experts who helped us update material for the revised edition: Marta Laughlin of Northwest Airlines, Angelo A. Nargo of Swissair, Allison Clements of Delta Airlines, Patricia Kelly of Amtrak, and Joi Mirsky of Garber Travel.

We extend our appreciation to the people who provided information on cruises and resorts: Deborah Weintraub-Roker of Sonesta International Hotels Corporation, Carrie Reckert of Hyatt Hotels and Resorts, Edwina Arnold of Club Med, Dinah Marzullo of Majesty Cruise Lines, and Jennifer Delacruise of Carnival Cruise Lines.

Our gratitude to all those who shared their travel experiences with us, especially Jennifer Roeper, Jill Bloom, Brenda Stern, Susan Dansker, Vesta Richardson, Lynne Bail, Cecelia Bohannon, Newell and Kate Flather, Cassandra Gaines, Roberta Idelson, Sheila Shulman, and Diane and Chris Welsh.

Our sincere thanks go to our original editor, Kathleen Cushman, who made us work harder than we thought we could and was repaid in kind; Linda Ziedrich, our editor for the revised edition; and Managing Editor Dan Rosenberg, for his help throughout. We are grateful as well to our agent, Helen Rees, who believed we had something worthwhile to say and helped make it possible for us to say it.

Finally, a loving thank-you to our family and friends for their continuing encouragement and support, and a special thanks to Tim, who suffered overburdened parents like a true champion.

CHAPTER ONE

The Pros and Cons of Family Travel

LET US START with a true confession. The idea for this book was born on a subway platform in Washington, DC, in the midst of a raging argument, during one of the most unsuccessful trips we have ever taken with our kids. Our daughter was not quite four; our son had just turned two.

We thought our vacation had been beautifully planned. We had driven from Boston to New York; the children complained in the car. We toured the city for two days; the children walked their little legs off. We drove from New York to Atlantic City and spent a sweltering day on the boardwalk; the children constantly demanded to be carried. We drove to Washington and checked into the third hotel in a week; the children never stopped fidgeting in restaurants. We were in the capital of our country, with nine thousand tourist attractions and four days to see them in, and we stood on this subway platform, tired, sweating, whining.

We were on vacation, but we didn't feel rested or relaxed; we felt like the slaves in Egypt, carrying stones to the top of a pyramid. We parents felt cheated; we both began to simmer; one of us yelled angrily, "I'm not having a good time!" and the other retorted, "Well, I'm not either!" That was the moment of recognition. Maybe, just maybe, we had not planned this trip quite carefully enough.

When we returned home, we began to discuss seriously what had gone wrong and why. To us it seemed odd: Both of us were experienced in working with children professionally, and one of us was a practicing psychologist who spent a great deal of time counseling others in methods of effective parenting. Up until now we had felt a lot of confidence in our own parenting instincts. In addition, we were both experienced travelers; we had been traveling with our children since our oldest was six weeks old. In short, we should have known better, we thought.

But what we had not done, in our haste to fit all this vacationing into a short period of time, was allow for the needs and limitations of our kids. As we eagerly thought about all the great things we would do, we had simply forgotten some basic things we knew about dealing with children. It was then that we began to interview other parents, talk to representatives of the travel industry, and conduct the other research that became the foundation for this book.

One fundamental fact became very clear: Traveling successfully with children requires thinking and planning. It's really not all that complicated. Much of it is common sense, as is much of parenting in general, although sometimes specific guidelines can be helpful. Overall, however, it is the attitude you bring to the planning of a family trip that makes all the difference. If you stop to think about what different members of the family would enjoy, what they are able to do, and what their limitations might be, your trip will probably be more fulfilling and more fun for everyone concerned.

No matter how you view yourself as a parent, thinking through your family travel plans can have very beneficial effects. If you feel that your relationship with your kids works beautifully and you travel with them very willingly, careful planning can work to make your trip even more enjoyable. If you are afraid that traveling with your children is too bumpy a road for you, then such planning may make the difference between being able to travel and staying home.

How you travel with your children is a matter of personal choice. Some families travel regularly, happily, and adventurously; we won't soon forget the humbling response of an acquaintance to whom we were eagerly describing our upcoming trip to the British Isles. "That sounds nice," she said. "Last year I took my kids up the Amazon. That was nice, too." Successful family excursions run the gamut from our Amazonian trekker to the family who rents the same familiar beach cottage every summer.

Families should go on the kinds of vacations that suit the parents and their children best.

For those parents who might travel with their kids if they felt more confident about it, we hope this book will give them that confidence. We would like, in addition, to expand the horizon both figuratively and literally for those parents who have kept their travel destinations limited, their wish to be more adventurous under control.

Finally, and primarily, we'd like to make family travel easier. As you go through this book you will find suggestions for planning and carrying out a trip from the earliest stages of deciding where to go to managing the little crises that invariably crop up (even better, we'll suggest how to keep little crises from cropping up too often). As you read our guidelines and concrete suggestions, please remember that we want to help you travel with *your* kids, not get you to travel as we do with ours. Adapt our ideas to your needs, your family, and your purposes. Use the general principles and advice to help plan the trip. Then carry this book with you to help your family get the most fun possible out of your vacation. We hope this book will help you to become wiser vacation planners and a successful traveling family for many trips to come.

Once you've thought of taking your kids along on your next vacation, you're obviously going to think next about what effects their presence will have. Will you really be able to enjoy the Louvre, or will all the paintings be a blur as you race through it? Will you be able to cover as many cities or countries as you'd like with the kids along? Such considerations come up all the time when parents think about traveling with their youngsters, and also when they try to decide where and how to travel.

There are, realistically, some limitations that you will face when taking the kids with you. But in our experience these limitations are rarely as overwhelming as parents imagine, and they are balanced by real benefits for both parents and children in traveling as a family. Maybe with the kids along you won't want to go to so many places on your trip, but you may get to know the places you do visit much better than you would otherwise. The whole trip may mean more to you, in fact, if you share it with your offspring. To help you consider what the tradeoffs will be, we'd like to first consider some of the more common concerns about taking the brood along, then try to separate the fantasy from the reality.

Common Apprehensions about Family Travel

There will be too many hassles; the trip won't be as relaxing. Well, there is certainly some truth to this. Any time you add to the number of people along, you add more temperaments and tastes to be accommodated. When those extra people are wholly dependent on you, then you will have some extra tasks to do. Generally, the best way to estimate the difficulty you are likely to have coping with your children's needs in hotels or campgrounds is by considering how you handle these needs at home. There is no reason to anticipate that little Johnny will become the Beast That Devoured Parenthood on vacation if he's generally manageable at home.

When in doubt, try it out. Take your child to a museum or to a nice, quiet restaurant near home if you plan to do so on your trip. This will give your child some practice at appropriate behavior in such circumstances, and give you an idea of her limits of tolerance.

We will have less freedom and flexibility. Yes, you will; and you should evaluate how important it is to you to be able to act on whim when you are on vacation. If you and your spouse feel the desire to nip out at midnight for a nightcap, you probably won't be able to if the kids are along. And you may need to keep to a schedule more than you would otherwise.

You needn't, however, feel trapped by your children. Babysitting can be arranged in many places. You can put the little ones to bed and order room service. And holding to rigid schedules may be unnecessary. Children are often more flexible about mealtimes and sleep times than adults give them credit for.

Taking our kids will limit where we can go. It will, but not so much as you may think. The more exotic your plans, the harder you should think about your children's capabilities and limitations. A backpacking trip in the foothills of the Himalayas with a two-year-old may be ill-conceived, and a trip geared to adult pleasures like museum hopping or theater going should be strictly for adults. But if you want to have a family vacation and feel that the needs of the kids are dictating where you should go, you are probably restricting the possibilities too much.

Stop and think what you personally want from this trip. If you give up too much, you're more likely to feel resentful and not to enjoy yourself. Expect that your kids will be able to give some; there is room to accommodate you, too, as you plan for a good balance in the trip's activities. Your kids' requirements should be viewed as one important factor among others in planning a trip. They should never be the sole determinant.

It's too expensive to take them along. Certainly taking more people costs more. But leaving your children behind might cost money, too, if you had to hire someone to stay home with them. Beyond the monetary outlay, you need to consider the emotional expense of leaving your children behind. If you would feel so guilty about going without them, or worry about them to the point of preoccupation, you would sacrifice your vacation in the process.

If you decide to bring the kids along despite the costs, then you can begin your search for low-cost family travel packages. Many are available these days; in fact, never before has the travel industry been more solicitous toward families or offered them more deals. Even if you're not interested in any of the package deals, you can figure out many ways of cutting down on expenses.

If you travel abroad, as of this writing each person is allowed to bring home $400 worth of articles duty-free. This includes children, so that a family of four has a $1,600 duty-free allowance. There are higher duty-free allowances for travelers returning from some countries in the Caribbean and Central America as well as some U.S. possessions. Check with your airlines or passport office before you go.

Parents need vacations away from their children. You bet they do! We intersperse trips by ourselves with family trips; the former tend to be of a different kind, geared to meeting our needs only. So don't feel guilty when you travel as a couple or singly—it's good for you. And when you do travel with the offspring, remember that childcare services are available almost everywhere. Some separateness is attainable even when you travel together.

Children are too young to get anything out of travel. As a general statement, this judgment is more often than not incorrect. Your children may not get the same things out of the trip that you will, but they will get a lot. Don't expect them to experience places as you do, but take care not to devalue the pleasures they will have, or underestimate what they may learn from a trip. The interest you show in the history of a place, or your appreciation of some cultural difference, may turn out to be more significant for your child than you would have imagined.

The Benefits of Family Travel

There is a lot more to traveling with your family than recreation or sightseeing. Traveling together can have varied and important effects on every family member.

Taking the kids along may enable you to travel more. Some people cut back on their travels once they have children because they think traveling with kids is too much of a hassle. But once you've decided to try taking the kids along, you may find yourselves traveling more than ever.

Travel is educational. For youngsters, travel is a firsthand learning experience that can be much more broadening than classroom lessons. Reading about Napoleon's conquests may be interesting, but standing beside the statue of the Lion of Waterloo and looking over the battlefield where he was defeated is an experience not easily forgotten. American history classes are useful, but standing in Ford's Theater and peering into the box where Lincoln was shot leaves a strikingly vivid impression. Such experiences, which may occur even on the least educational-sounding trip, can make class lessons really meaningful. The child recently returned from collecting shells at the beach will feel more personally involved, for instance, in a science unit on the oceans.

This sort of learning doesn't stop with the young ones. You too will find that your trips are more educational with the kids along. Explaining the westward movement of the American pioneers will make your own experience of the American West much richer. And as you tour the Tower of London and listen alongside your children while the Beefeater explains what happened there, those kings and queens of your own school days will come so much more vividly into focus.

> *Take a few special books that involve the region where you're traveling, to read aloud to the whole family. D'Aulaire's book of Greek myths, the Laura Ingalls Wilder books, the tales of King Arthur will all take on a special dimension in their particular settings.*

It's not just a greater appreciation of history and the physical world that makes the travel experience educational. An increased awareness of different customs and attitudes can make the whole family more wise and sensitive.

Travel stimulates personal growth. As they experience new people and places, children become more curious to learn, more open to new events and ideas. It's as if they expand their outlooks to accommodate their growing world. By personally experiencing the differences among peoples or among the vast varieties of physical environments, they develop some perspective on their own place in the larger world. Traveling within the United States gives children an idea of how large and diverse our country is; coming back from less developed countries results in a greater understanding of what it means to live here. Your children may develop more sensitivity to other people and to other points of view, and better understand their own place in the world.

Finally, when you travel you will all constantly confront new challenges. You may make your way through the Belgian countryside without speaking a word of French or Flemish, barter for some prized object in a flea market in Madrid, or make friends with a German child in the campground at Yellowstone. As your children meet each challenge, they will learn that they can manage in the world around them, and gain a sense of competence and self-confidence that may last a lifetime.

Kids learn practical skills while traveling. Travel can stimulate a child's start in acquiring a great many skills. Those first few words of French may open the way for studying foreign languages, and the child who is already learning one in school can increase his fluency when he travels. An understanding of how to handle

> *If your children have permission to use your first names in an emergency, it's easier for them to locate you in a crowd; "Norman!" or "Norman Posner!" is more likely to get your attention than one more little one calling, "Daddy!"*

money can arise from the rapt interest many children show in foreign currencies and their denominations. Unexpected events can provide practical lessons in problem solving. Map reading, orienteering, climbing, and hiking techniques are but a few of the endless variety of useful abilities travel can teach. In short, it's hard to go to new places and have new experiences without picking up some skills that will be valuable in the future.

Traveling with children is a richer experience for parents. You'll simply notice more with the kids along. Children have an exuberance and an uninhibited appreciation for simple things that more "worldly" folks might overlook. If only to entertain them, you'll notice birds, flowers, insects, and foliage that you might otherwise pass by without noticing. That tiny, ramshackle aquarium behind a gift shop in a small beach resort, which looked like five minutes' worth of entertainment for the kids, may turn out to have a delightful collection of seals to feed. You really will get to know places better, and come home with some memories you'd never have if you hadn't taken the kids.

Then there are kids' questions: How did this get here? Why is it like this? Coming up with the answers can make you stop and think about where you are, and take a greater interest in what you are seeing.

Children bring an infectious joie de vivre to travel. At their best, your children can provide unanticipated moments of laughter and pleasure. One of our warmest memories of San Francisco is of our two-year-old son's glee as he chased pigeons through Golden Gate Park. How well we remembered a similar scene three years earlier, when our daughter, then one, had joyfully chased New Brunswick pigeons through a Canadian campground. We adults may look at, breathe in, and immerse ourselves in a new place; but children seem able to become a part of it.

Travel brings the family closer together. There is something about sharing the pleasures and the tribulations of a journey that produces real feelings of togetherness. Maybe it is sharing the wonder of discovery, or acquiring memories to be pulled out and examined together for years to come. Maybe seeing one another in new situations and in new lights actually helps you get to know each other better. Whatever the reasons, the effect is a sense of cohesiveness that becomes a permanent part of the growth and healthy functioning of the family.

> *Send your child a postcard from her own trip, timed to arrive a few days after you all return home. ("Having a great time—glad you were here!") This will help relieve the post-trip back-to-boredom blues.*

Children act as goodwill ambassadors. Most kids lack the inhibitions adults have when it comes to meeting others. They make new friends in campgrounds, motel swimming pools, just about anywhere. And because they tend to be naturally outgoing, you too will invariably meet more people during your travels. Adults with and without children are often drawn to little ones, and people will frequently be exceptionally kind and helpful when you are with your kids. Thus your opportunities will increase to experience in a very personal way the cultures and temperaments of the people through whose lands you are traveling.

These are some of the good things that can happen when you travel with your kids. With them, we think, you will discover not only more excitement and pleasure during your journey together, but also an immeasurable and permanent change in the quality of your family life and your feelings about yourselves.

CHAPTER TWO

Different Kids at Different Ages

WE HAVE ADVISED YOU to take into account your children's capacities as you think about what kind of trip to take. This shouldn't be the factor around which you plan, and you certainly should never ignore your own preferences, but looking realistically at your kids is important in planning a healthy balance of activities on your trip. So we will describe here major developmental stages as they may affect your child's behavior during your travels.

The outline of developmental events here is very broad. We divide childhood into five stages, each encompassing some years, and highlight a few major changes that can affect the travel experience. We make no attempt to be comprehensive, and, for heaven's sake, don't use this outline to check out whether your child is developing normally! Among entirely normal children, there is a lot of overlap from one stage to another. What one child does at two another won't achieve until a year later. Your child is unique, so the general points here will apply well in some areas, not as well in others. As you plan your trip, your knowledge about your child should override our knowledge about kids in general.

The Infant (Birth to 18 Months)

This is obviously the period when the child most depends on the parents to meet his needs, and when he has the fewest independent abilities. An infant can be easy to take along, especially in the early months; you can attend to his basic needs just about anywhere. He'll probably sleep a lot, which he can do nestled comfortably in a sling or other carrier or in a reclining stroller. As long as you plan for the additional burden, city touring on foot or wilderness hiking can be much easier with an infant than with a slightly older child.

You will of course need to allow time for feeding and changing breaks, and you may want to check ahead about the availability of cribs where you will be staying. Even if the baby is very young, plan for some time and space to accommodate her desire to move. As movement increases from creeping to standing with support to unsteady walking, you should intersperse quiet times with opportunities for the baby to practice the new locomotion and experience the periodic frustrations that go with it. A six-month-old can be transported in a pack or stroller most of the day, but an eighteen-month-old will demand some time to romp, whether in a hotel room, city park, or campground. She'll be pretty good about going where you want to go, but you'll have to slow down and let her use her own feet once in a while.

Stranger or separation anxiety may appear at around nine months or a bit later. While it lasts, it will be less problematic on trips with fewer transitions and new faces, and the security of your constant presence.

Since this is the period of most limited speech, you will have to anticipate your child's needs. At a year to a year and a half she will probably use speech only for rudimentary communication, indicating a whole thought in one word rather than a phrase or sentence. Often this is enough, but sometimes your child will get frustrated at her inability to make herself understood. During this period just before language is a truly useful tool, many parents prefer to stay away from restaurants and other settings that demand a lot of self-control. Others go ahead and take their kids to such places, but adjust their expectations accordingly.

The Toddler (Ages 1½ to 3)

The rapid development of speech during this period helps greatly when you travel with your child. He will probably be able to tell you what he wants and ask questions, and he'll comprehend your answers better. (You may question whether it is an advantage to have your child tell you in words that he won't eat instead of grunting, but maybe he'll also be able to tell you what he *will* eat.) By three years he'll probably have quite a large vocabulary, and the broadening experience of travel may promote even faster language development.

Still, little Henry may not always be able to verbalize what's bothering him. Especially when he is tired, the words aren't always readily available, and sometimes it's just easier to whine or cry. So you will need to try to anticipate overtiring situations, but you will also need to listen carefully and patiently to what he does try to say. Be buttressed by the knowledge that, more and more, he will be able to tell you what's up.

Attention span and frustration tolerance are both limited at this age. Lengthy visits to museums and other activities requiring quiet and concentration can be problematic. Don't skip them, but consider shortening your stays; see that art exhibit on a couple of occasions for an hour at a time rather than trying to take it all in at once. Changing the pace or kind of activity may help to avoid whines. Follow the White House tour, for instance, with a trip to the national zoo, where your child can run and yell in the open air.

This is a stage at which children begin to try their wings a bit, boldly asserting themselves and then running back to the safety of the parents. Your child may express her urge for independence in various ways, none of which will be very different when traveling from when you're at home. At times you will find your two-year-old demanding, battling to see who's in control, or acting contrary for the mere pleasure of giving you a hard time. Although this behavior may be nothing new, it can be especially trying when you are supposed to be on vacation. You'll need to remember that the behavior is normal, and to respond to it essentially as you would at home, by setting some gentle but firm limits.

The other side of the coin in the toddler's struggle for autonomy is the tendency to become clingy and dependent at times. This may happen most when the child has been bombarded with newness—new settings, people, foods, experiences. He may balk at going sightseeing again or have trouble adjusting to a new bed. Again, don't panic. Reassuring words and hugs will help, as will your constant presence; this may not be a good time to leave your child with an unfamiliar babysitter. Having a favorite teddy bear or similar valued object from home can also be very calming and reassuring to your toddler.

Toddlers still have limited motor capacities, may have incomplete bowel and bladder control, and are liable to tire easily. Take these things into consideration in deciding where to go (hiking the Appalachian Trail?) and in planning the day's itinerary. Short rest stops will help a great deal. A good backpack may be handy for walking in all sorts of terrain, and a stroller can be a godsend in cities (even if you have stopped using a stroller at home, consider using it for heavy-duty walking; it will not undo your parenting, and it may practically eliminate complaining). Whenever a bathroom is handy, ask if your child needs to go (sometimes it seems children are born with a sixth sense that tells them when they are at the farthest point from a bathroom so that they can tell their parents that they have to go). Expect that a bathroom stop will be needed soon after each meal. A child recently toilet-trained may regress temporarily while traveling, so if you're not certain of your child's continence, bring along some disposable diapers, especially for nighttimes, and keep a change of clothes handy. Some parents find they can prevent accidents by bringing their children's familiar potty chair on family trips.

We tend to be a bit more lenient on the road than we would be at home; our kids know that they're going to get away with having fewer vegetables and more soda with dinner when we are on vacation. We admit unabashedly that we relax restrictions this way for one reason: to make things easier on ourselves. We don't worry that a little extra leeway at times will destroy our child rearing in the long run. So don't let your limit setting ruin your good time; go ahead and ease up. It's even okay to bargain a bit (my historical site followed by your playground), within reasonable bounds (never "Please can we go to the historical site?").

The Pre-Schooler (Ages 3 to 5)

During the pre-school years, the child's awareness of the world begins to widen. She can understand more about people and events outside the family circle and how they relate to her. Kids at this age become more conscious of differences among people, places, and ways of life. Most also start to become more sociable.

Children are more eager at this age for new experiences, and find more meaning in visiting new places. You may be able to bargain with your child a bit more, to gain his cooperation during one activity while he awaits another more to his liking. But you'll still need to emphasize varied and short-span activities to keep your child's interest high.

This is even more than before a period of fluctuating attempts to be autonomous, but with an overall trend toward reaching out independently. Your child will discover how the use of language and social skills opens new vistas for her, and she will delight in using these skills. But once in a while, too, she'll probably retreat, returning to the umbrella of your protection, reminding you that she is still little and needs to be taken care of. Don't be overly concerned about clingy behavior; you needn't cancel the rest of the vacation because the trip seems to be too much for your child. Just be there to cuddle her when she needs you to, encourage her to do things for herself when she can, and be patient with the phases that come and go.

A child's physical capabilities are usually well established by this time. But although your child may be able to walk several miles at a stretch, you'll still need to respect the shortness of his legs and the ease with which he tires. Nap time may still be an important part of the daily schedule. Use it to your advantage (get in some driving time, have a family siesta, or give each other turns getting out alone). Well-developed speech will make it easier for your child to make his feelings understood, and his increased comprehension will add to the excitement of discovering and enjoying things together. Finally, though your child will hopefully have left the diaper stage, you may need to remind him to go to the bathroom when one is handy, and help him manage in public restrooms.

Middle Childhood (Ages 5 to 10)

Physical restrictions are pretty much by the board now. Most motor skills are well developed by about six, and strength and stamina should also be greatly increased. Physically demanding trips, whether hiking or urban touring, are more feasible now. But be aware of your child's particular physical abilities, and remember that he may not be able to keep pace with an adult.

A child's awareness of herself as an individual, separate from her parents, takes on real importance during this stage of development. This is a time for a child to enter new relationships, to figure out who she is in relation to others. For this reason, travel may at this age finally be termed "broadening" in the adult sense. The child over five handles cultural differences better, and learns more about herself and others by meeting people from varied places.

Kids during these years are generally more outgoing than younger children, and they take some initiative for making things happen. Your child may take an active role in planning and carrying out the trip, making suggestions that may lead the whole family into memorable moments. The satisfaction of completing a canoe trip or mastering the use of chopsticks will result in increasing self-confidence. Your child's ability to read, when he acquires it, will add to the whole family's enjoyment of a trip, as he shares what he has read about the place you're visiting or reads menus and orders his own meals in restaurants. Books or magazines will keep your child quiet, too, when he is bored or needs a break.

When a child reaches seven or eight, she may become preoccupied with rules (this is that lovely age at which your children begin to remind you of your minor indiscretions: "Daddy, you didn't put any money in the parking meter"). Concerns about good and bad and right and wrong manifest themselves; kids this age will pay more attention to appropriateness in all of its various forms. As you travel, they will have questions about differences they experience; they will be curious about propriety and demand to know "what's right." From your patient explanations they will learn and grow. This is, of course, the most fun for you when your offspring asks those inevitable questions that require about three weeks' worth of explanation ("To them, *we're* the ones with the funny accent . . .").

Play during this stage can often be structured into games;

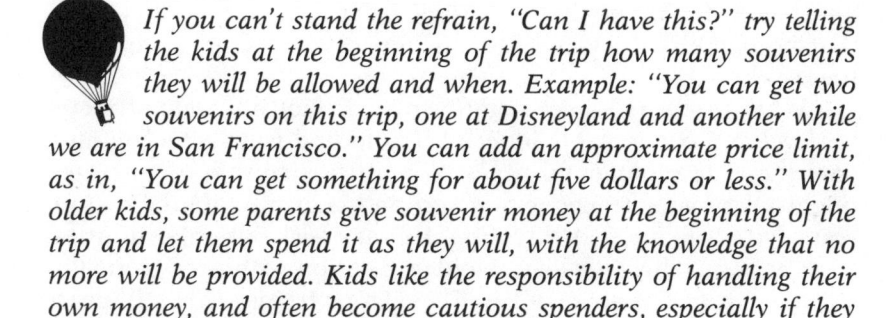

If you can't stand the refrain, "Can I have this?" try telling the kids at the beginning of the trip how many souvenirs they will be allowed and when. Example: "You can get two souvenirs on this trip, one at Disneyland and another while we are in San Francisco." You can add an approximate price limit, as in, "You can get something for about five dollars or less." With older kids, some parents give souvenir money at the beginning of the trip and let them spend it as they will, with the knowledge that no more will be provided. Kids like the responsibility of handling their own money, and often become cautious spenders, especially if they can keep whatever money is left at the end.

there is not as much need for yelling and running wildly (though some room to cavort is still welcome once in a while). This means easier times in hotel rooms, planes, cars, and restaurants, where you can use coloring books or guessing games to pass the time.

Kids this age have greater self-control than younger ones. Since they can remain calm for longer periods, are increasingly patient, and lack some of their earlier fears, the range of activities you can all do together expands. You can go to museums that aren't "hands-on," for instance, or enjoy slow, quiet restaurant meals. And since kids this age generally don't need naps and can dress and groom themselves, you can plan a fuller travel schedule.

Puberty and Adolescence

As a child begins his final dash toward adulthood, struggles for autonomy recur. These may be mostly internal, as the preadolescent and adolescent argues with himself about replacing his parents' values with his own; or he may act out these struggles in a seemingly endless battle of wills with his mother and father. His behavior may be erratic, while traveling as well as at other times.

To begin with, your adolescent may be disinclined to go with you at all; this is an option that should be given some consideration if alternative arrangements are possible. She may vacillate about going, changing her mind repeatedly. Tell her you'd like to have her with you (if you really would), and try to communicate some understanding for her reluctance. If she does come along, she'll probably feel the need to be off on her own at times, or to experience things in a very individual way. Until now you may have been used to having all members of the family agree easily on what to do, but no more. Your teenager may want to do things that no one else does and never seem to want to go along with the family.

What seems like sheer negativism is, in fact, a sincere attempt to develop a comfortable identity. Try to find ways to accommodate these developmental urges. When it seems safe to you, you might allow your teenager to go off on his own while the rest of you head off in another direction. He may seek out opportunities to meet people his own age; the identification with peer groups is a large part of this stage of life. This can be trying—you still need to set firm limits, to use your parental discretion so as to not allow your child to engage in irresponsible or dangerous behavior, but you simultaneously want to respect his uniqueness. Achieving this balance is another factor to consider while on the road.

During the adolescent years, youngsters are able to interpret new experiences on a more abstract level. Travel becomes educational in an even broader way as they become more aware of different value systems, develop a sense of history, or compare the similarities and variations among ethnic groups. They discover ideas as well as sights and sounds. Sharing these discoveries may provide a few precious moments of unity between you and your teenager.

The Guinness Book of World Records is a good travel companion for the eight- to thirteen-year-old.

CHAPTER THREE

Planning Your Trip

A VACATION usually represents one of the largest expenditures in the family budget. Yet there is often less thought put into it than into what kind of refrigerator to buy. You may choose a destination after browsing through the Sunday travel section, or on the basis of a quick suggestion by your neighborhood travel agent, or because it has been the family vacation spot since the Great Blizzard of '33. Plans are made, everyone fantasizes for weeks ahead about the wonderful things they will see or do, and at last the trip happens.

And then comes an odd reaction—no one is really satisfied. The vacation turns out not quite as expected; something was missing; you had an okay time, but. . . .

Such disgruntled reactions can be avoided; all you need do is think ahead about what you want to get out of your journey. People often go on trips for the wrong reasons, or they neglect to gear a trip to their specific requirements.

The idea of trying to please five or six people with one vacation may sound complicated, but it isn't. You just have to go at it in a systematic way. Let us go through each phase of this decision-making process.

Deciding What You Want from This Trip

It's easy to go to a place that doesn't provide what you need—especially if you weren't really aware what you or your children needed in the first place. A two-thousand-mile automobile tour may sound exciting, but it's not for you if you've been feeling drained at work and you need peace and calm. Lying around at the beach may be just the thing for a frazzled Mommy or Daddy, but not really rejuvenating if you've been feeling dull, listless, and in need of stimulation. You'll need to know not only what sort of experiences generally suit your style, but also what you most hanker for right now, as you plan this trip.

Let's begin by looking at some of the general purposes that travel and vacations can serve. Afterward, we will look at how these may apply to your whole family; but for the moment just think about what an individual can glean from traveling. Keep in mind as you read that any one trip will serve a number of functions and supply a variety of experiences. An African safari can provide for change, entertain you, tax your muscles, and make you feel adventurous—all very distinct benefits. As you get ready to go on vacation, what kinds of benefits do you feel you most need from the trip?

Rest and relaxation. Recharging one's run-down batteries is one of the most common reasons for going away. How you do it, and where you do it, depends on your own particular style. You can rest by swinging in a hammock in the backyard, listening to the birds on the deck of an A-frame in the woods, or baking in the sun with surf crashing nearby. For one person relaxation means sleeping as late as she wants to, for another it means having no schedules to keep or no meals to cook. We know an accountant who takes a week off every year as soon as tax season ends. His vacation has only one purpose, relaxation—which for him includes getting up at 6:00 A.M. to play tennis before breakfast. Since he seems normal in most ways, we assume that if he says that's relaxing for him, then it is. For most people, however, rest and relaxation means having more time to loaf, no matter how they choose to do it.

Physical invigoration. For some, a vacation means the opportunity to renew acquaintance with one's body. Stretching one's own physical limits after months of sitting behind a desk provides an exhilarating sense of renewal. For such folks, challenging nature often goes hand in hand with challenging themselves. These are the people who will use their vacations to go white-water canoeing or rock climbing, or to hike the Appalachian Trail; as they refresh their bodies, they renew their spirits as well. Teenagers often enjoy taking on such challenges along with their parents. There are other, less herculean, ways to have a strenuous physical vacation, of course. A week at a tennis camp or a dude ranch can leave you feeling alive and strong and just sore enough to know that you've been there.

> *If your family will do a lot of walking or hiking on your trip, you may all need to work on improving your strength and stamina before you go. But keep the warmups enjoyable, or you'll be less than eager to set out on a vacation ramble!*

Replenishing the soul. This may sound a bit grandiose, but some trips can provide spiritual invigoration without the physical exertions just described. Viewing the wonders of nature can be such an experience. Standing at the edge of the Grand Canyon can be mind expanding, as can surveying a panorama from atop a mountain peak. Each year around February or early March, after a long winter of gloomy days and indoor activities, our family hungers to see the ocean. We pack ourselves into the car, and then we stand on a beach or a rocky crag watching the late winter wind whip the foam and buffet us; what this does for our spirits is indescribable. Such experiences inspire introspection, bringing one closer in touch with oneself. Lying on the grass on a clear summer night and gazing into a star-filled heaven can produce a sense of awe and peace, a feeling of perspective and understanding that is a major benefit of this type of vacation.

Entertainment. Ah, hedonistic pleasure! And what better time to indulge than on vacation? Finding a spot to satisfy this need primarily means looking for the best place to play, to indulge oneself, to be taken care of. This can happen in a resort, or in a city where you stay in a good hotel, take in shows, and dine at restaurants. You may feel the need to have other people around doing things for you, or to find a setting that offers an assortment of activities or events designed to amuse you.

Educational or cultural enrichment. Time off means intellectual stimulation to some people; for them the thrill of learning is an exhilarating part of the travel experience. Such intellectual adventurers may be drawn to historical sites, where they can immerse themselves in tradition or study battle strategies. They might take in museums, symphonies, or ballets. Or they may use vacation time to take that wine-tasting or folk-dancing course they've been attracted to for so long. Foreign travel provides learning experiences even if no formal cultural events are scheduled into the trip. Firsthand exposure to different societies is the best way to broaden one's experience and perspective.

Adventure. The dictionary defines adventure as "an unusual, stirring experience, often of a romantic nature." What determines such an experience? Again, this depends on who you are; whereas one adventurer may want to explore the Galapagos Islands, another may be satisfied by motoring across the United States. For the most part, though, those who seek adventure take more exotic trips, and bring together fantasy and reality in a very satisfying way. Having a drink amidst the bazaars of Marrakech or riding a mule down a steep trail in the Grand Canyon may provide just the excitement or romance to relieve worries about the broken water heater at home. And stories from an adventurous vacation can keep the conversation going at parties (or, for your kids, at recess) for the next year.

Escape. Whenever we ask people what they look for in vacations, a lot of them name this elusive little item. The major ingredient sought after here is change—of setting, pace, or routine. Such changes are one of the main reasons behind any vacation. But the escapist vacationer has a special hazard to be aware of: Without realizing it, she may be trying to escape from some unhappiness within herself. The couple in the midst of domestic turmoil who go off with the kids on vacation may believe that they will enjoy each other more on St. Martin than they do at home in Cleveland. But along with the camera and clothes they pack up their resentments and hostilities, and their vacation becomes one more disappointment to fuel the fire. Travel can indeed provide some relief from tension and the chance to refocus one's energy and attention and even to make important changes. But it cannot cure unhappiness in a family or boredom and frustration with one's life in general.

Family togetherness. Traveling can provide a chance for a family to grow closer, to get to know one another better. For those who value family togetherness beyond all other goals of vacation, the best trips provide shared activities that reflect the styles and preferences of the people involved. Listening together to the sounds of bagpipes echoing in the Scottish Highlands may satisfy some, whereas others may prefer to play Frisbee on the beach. Taking day trips from home can achieve this benefit as well as a month's touring in a recreational vehicle; but a trip to a city where the parents will pursue adult activities on their own won't do at all.

Visiting friends or relatives. For many people, vacation time is for renewing family bonds, for giving Grandma and Grandpa a chance to see how the little ones have grown or to "spoil" them a little. Such visits can reestablish links with the past, refresh one's view of the family as a generational process, and provide essential time with the people you love. In their own way, trips like this can be among the most energizing and renewing.

Deciding What's Right for Your Family

Okay, you've sorted through the different purposes that travel can serve. The first thing you'll want to do is toss out those vacation ideas that just don't seem right to you and your family. Be realistic. If you abhor visiting friends and relatives it would make no sense to spend your precious vacation time doing so. If you find it hard to function without creature comforts, then the foothills of the Himalayas may not be your bag. But for every family there will remain a set of varied possibilities. The question is this: Which benefits are most important to you at this point in your lives?

First, ask yourself what life has been like for your family recently. Has it been so demanding that some or all of you feel drained? Have you or the children been feeling bored and in need of something different? Has the cabin fever of a long winter made the sun seem like some fabled mythological object? In other words, what's cooking at this point in your lives that needs response?

Then add to the mixture some questions about the kinds of people you are. Are you a close-knit family who enjoy doing all sorts of things together, or do you prefer to go in different directions? Are your kids on the quiet side, liking to read or watch television, or are they high-energy types who need to keep moving? Ask the same questions about you and your spouse; are different members of the family different in these regards? Don't forget to ask yourself what you all like to do, whether separately or together. Once you've rattled these questions around, you'll have a better general idea of what might belong on your travel agenda. You can then begin to consider how your family would react to various types of trips. How do those different travel benefits we discussed apply to your own family's personalities and needs? Let's look at some examples.

* During the past year the Carsons have moved to a new part of the country. The children are still in the process of making new friends and adjusting to their new school, and both Frank and Eleanor Carson are making the difficult adaptation to the demands of their new jobs. The past three months have been spent with a decorator who seems to want the Carsons' new house to look like the summer palace of the Hapsburgs, and half the family's moving boxes are still not unpacked.

As summer approaches, the Carsons begin to plan their annual family vacation. Eleanor's sister wants them to come with her on a bargain eleven-country tour of Europe; a colleague of Frank's is suggesting a white-water rafting trip down the Colorado River; and their new neighbors have a cottage on the beach that they're willing to rent to the Carsons. What should they do?

The Carsons like to travel; several times in years past they have taken the family on successful big-city vacations. But is this the year for them to tour eleven European countries in as many days? Better they should send the decorator. And though they like a beautiful view as much as anyone, Eleanor Carson can't face the prospect of making camp along the Colorado each evening for two weeks. "I feel as if I've been camping in my own kitchen for long enough," she says. All things considered, come holiday time the Carsons had better head for their neighbor's ocean cottage and sit awhile. Several factors—recent events, their current feelings, and the styles and attitudes of the people involved—combine to make two quiet weeks at the beach the Carsons' choice this year.

* The MacGregor family has a different dilemma to work out. Helen MacGregor is a history professor at the local university; her husband, Alex, works as a software engineer. Their tenth-grade son has just won the city-wide science fair for the working Roman water clock he made, and his sister is the top gymnast on her high-school team. Helen is a member of the town council, Alex chairman of the local committee for the arts. The MacGregor

children have been active in scouting for years and are now scout leaders for younger children. On weekends, the family likes to go on long bicycle trips together; they are active members of the art museum, the science museum, and the aquarium.

Here is a family energized by intellectual stimulation, always active, intensely curious, and rarely bored. Should they spend their upcoming vacation visiting Aunt Emma in Peoria, Illinois? With all due respect to Peoria, this would probably be a mistake for the MacGregors (better they should send the Carsons' decorator). They do, however, enjoy strenuous exercise, the beauties of nature, and family togetherness, though they go their own ways as well. Educational and cultural enrichment, too, rank high in their priorities.

Under ordinary circumstances the MacGregors might decide to take a trip that satisfied as many of those interests as possible. That intercollegiate archeological dig in the Mideast could be perfect for them, they think. But hold on a moment. Helen MacGregor has spent the past year writing a book on Minoan civilization; frankly, she says, she's had it up to her ears with archeology. Better scratch that dig. How about camping in the Southwest? They could combine the great outdoors with some Indian culture; it's a trip they've always wanted to make. Oh, but wait. The past month has produced the hottest June in history; the MacGregors are already shriveled by the scorching heat. So maybe a little rock climbing in the cool green mountains of Vermont? Like the Carsons, the MacGregors have arrived at this decision by combining what suits their own personalities and temperaments with a vacation that meets some specific current needs.

- Unlike the Carsons and the MacGregors, the Feldstein family is a rather disparate bunch, so different from one another that one wonders how they manage to live together. Dan Feldstein is the adventurous type, a spontaneous fellow who can be off on a whim, never bothered by not having planned ahead. In his early twenties he hitchhiked across Asia just for the fun of it. His wife, Cindy, in sharp contrast, is orderly and exacting, an excellent planner and organizer; she takes care to see that family life is as comfortable as possible. At five, their son Paul is a healthy boy with varied interests. Just now, however, Paul is suffering through one of those developmental transitions of childhood; he wakes up frightened at night, finds it difficult to separate from his parents, and seems easily startled.

This week Dan Feldstein came across a vacation idea that has awakened his old sense of adventure. In the back of a travel magazine he spotted an ad for a wagon train adventure through the American Southwest—complete with Conestoga wagon, campfire cooking, even a surprise Indian attack or two (no kidding, this trip package exists!). But Cindy reacts with something less than enthusiasm. Outhouses and outlaws are not her idea of a relaxing break. What suits her more is a civilized sojourn where she can be waited on for a change—a resort in the Poconos, perhaps, with a few shows, a little shuffleboard, and plenty of great food. And how about young Paul? Is this a good year for him to enjoy dramatic changes and surprise Indian attacks?

The Feldsteins may not be able to suit everybody's tastes perfectly this year; for them, the trick will be to accommodate everyone to some degree. Perhaps a cruise would fit the bill: for Cindy relaxation, service, civility, and food, food, food; for Paul a lot of time with his parents in peaceful, unchanging surroundings; and for adventurous Dan a little romance on the moonlit Caribbean.

Almost any traveling family will sometimes find themselves in situations like this, when they must plan a vacation with something to suit people's different needs. Everything from your individual tastes to your personality styles and the ages of the kids will be factors in choosing what to do. Once you've identified the major purposes you personally want your trip to serve, ask yourselves whether each family member has the same needs, or other important ones. Ask each family member what they need from this vacation. Even younger kids will be able to tell you, though you may have to translate their specific requests into the kinds of more abstract goals we've been talking about.

As we have seen, it is possible to integrate different goals into one trip. In order to do so, first you will have to choose priorities, and then you will have to compromise. Rank the different requirements family members have of this vacation in order of their relative importance—even though your judgments are subjective,

Favorite activities for children on any kind of trip often involve (1) heights, (2) water, (3) unusual modes of transportation, (4) animals, or (5) any combination of these.

they will be of help. Once you have a list of priorities, think about which goals are essential for a successful trip and which might be dropped to satisfy other demands. Don't give up your parental discretion in deciding what you think your kids need. You are the parent, and your judgment is needed here.

Analyzing Your Choices

At this point, you can begin to zero in on an actual decision about where and how to go. Now that you have some ideas about your family's travel needs, what are your choices? With thousands of settings and events to choose from, this can be an intimidating prospect. Unless you have spent considerable time traveling, your own repertory of ideas may be somewhat limited. But perspectives can be broadened, and all sorts of ideas can be stimulated by tapping into various sources.

Talk first among yourselves. There are times when you will need no sources beyond this. You may have a favorite spot that you all feel is just the tonic you need. Or you may very quickly hit upon an idea that makes everyone happy. But at other times you may need to put your heads together and sound out various people's ideas. Even if no one has specific recommendations, the exchange of ideas will stimulate new possibilities.

Be sure to include the kids in this conversation, and listen carefully to their suggestions. Even a four-year-old, with a limited awareness of geography, can come up with something that will set off an association in your mind. A teenager who's into reggae or who knows an exchange student from Trinidad may have ideas for a Caribbean trip. And children of all ages are capable of saying "Let's go back to the seashore," or "Let's go someplace new."

Talk to friends. Friends who have traveled to different places with their families can be especially helpful. Ask them to describe what those places were like, what the families did, what was good and bad about their trips. Ask if they would mind showing you their slides. (Have you ever known anyone who minded showing their travel slides? This request will probably cement your friendship for life.) Ask the questions that mean the most for your family. If your friends have been camping in a wilderness area and you know your family would need an occasional break during that kind of a trip, ask whether there is a town nearby and what one can do there.

Treat friends' suggestions only as a starting place, however. Specific suggestions don't always transfer well from one family to another; your trip may differ quite a bit from your neighbor's to the same place, whether you are camping in upstate New York, spending a week in San Francisco, or cruising on the Rhine. Listen for general ideas about places to check out, not for concrete notions about what the experience will be like for your clan. And remember that another family can report only their own limited experiences; what they have seen and done may not represent all possibilities.

Just before our first trip to Europe, a friend who had once spent a week in Vienna during a summer cool spell warned us to take along overcoats; "Europe is cold," she said confidently of an entire continent. One friend asserts that Martha's Vineyard is a terrible place to take children because there is little to do besides go to the beach; another friend sees this same spot as ideal for his family—for exactly the same reason.

Read travel articles. Newspapers and magazines can be good sources of ideas for trips; we read them routinely, and clip articles for future reference as well as immediate vacation plans. We save articles about places we already like, about any that appeal to a particular interest of ours, or about trips that just sound particularly intriguing. This file can then be consulted whenever ideas for a trip are needed.

Both travel magazines and travel sections in Sunday newspapers tend to have their own particular personalities; some are geared toward business travelers or those seeking luxury, whereas others aim to please a broader group of readers. Local newspapers and regional magazines are especially good sources of inexpensive vacation ideas, since they tend to emphasize possibilities within the region. Even parenting magazines and newspapers often carry travel articles, and these are sometimes the most relevant to those who travel with children. Whatever your sources, they can serve as a continuing supply of good ideas. Remember to watch for useful addresses so you can obtain further information when you need it.

Gather information from tourist offices. Almost all industrialized countries, all of the U.S. states, and many cities publish brochures and other printed information designed to attract tourism. In addition, many foreign countries maintain tourist offices in the United States (the main ones are usually in New York City), from which you can request information. Travel agencies and auto clubs can provide addresses and phone numbers of local and foreign tourist offices; to find out how to reach a state tourist office, call the state house. The quality of tourist literature varies greatly, but an inquiry usually brings illustrated descriptions of the region and a calendar of events. Be as specific as possible in asking for what you want; the tourist office may be the most complete source of information about an area, from its weather patterns to its train fares, but to be most helpful the staff must know what you're interested in.

Read travel books. A bookstore with a good travel section is a rich mine of ideas and information all laid out for you in a colorful array. These books may be the best source for exploring vacation possibilities; there are books on just about every region of the world, books aimed at business travelers, budget travelers, camping buffs, and bicyclists. Just browsing through the titles can stimulate all sorts of ideas, and a little skimming can quickly tell you whether further research is warranted. Libraries can also be good places to explore travel ideas, although the books may be out of date.

Once you get to your destination, stop by the tourist office or visitors' center to scoop up as many pamphlets about restaurants, lodgings, entertainment, and special attractions as you can carry; usually, there are so many such pamphlets to choose from that they're mailed only on specific request. Many of these pamphlets will amount to little more than advertisements for the establishments that printed them, but you may discover some pearls you might have missed otherwise. Also look for an up-to-date listing of special events for the week or month you will be in the area; hotels, motels, and shops may also have such a list available.

Consult travel agents. Picking the brain of a good travel agent is an excellent first step towards choosing the right trip for your family. You need not be ready to buy when you visit an agency. Simply explain what your family requires in the way of a vacation, and ask what recommendations the agent can make. No matter how honest you are about not being ready to buy, an agent's first purpose will be to sell you something. Still, while you are shopping for ideas it is to an agent's advantage to talk with you and try to answer your questions; if the agent seems to have a variety of creative ideas or knows a lot about family travel, you may come back to that person when it's time for specific arrangements.

Agents specialize in prepackaged travel arrangements such as tours, so the suggestions they are able to make may actually be more limited than your own ideas. Also, many agents don't do much family travel planning, so you may have to evaluate their suggestions in light of your own knowledge about family needs. Nonetheless, a good travel agent will have ideas and experience regarding a wide range of places; and you may find one who has traveled extensively with his or her own family.

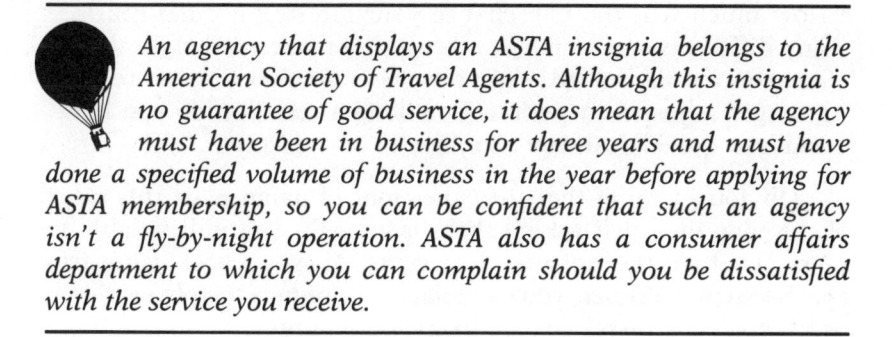

An agency that displays an ASTA insignia belongs to the American Society of Travel Agents. Although this insignia is no guarantee of good service, it does mean that the agency must have been in business for three years and must have done a specified volume of business in the year before applying for ASTA membership, so you can be confident that such an agency isn't a fly-by-night operation. ASTA also has a consumer affairs department to which you can complain should you be dissatisfied with the service you receive.

Time to Decide

By this time you should have in mind a few trips with the ingredients of a successful family vacation. The ideas you came up with at your family meeting now have more shape and substance, and more information to back them up. Now you can call the family together again to sort through your ideas and make a selection.

This is a good time to remind yourself that there is no correct family vacation. You know your family and your own style better than anyone; plan accordingly. Specifically, don't foreclose on possibilities just because they lack special kid-appeal; children are not all the same in their abilities, interests, and adaptability. And if you all feel drawn to a particular vacation, even if it is not the most logical choice, don't be afraid to go with it.

Finally, run your choice through a checklist to make sure that its potential for success is high.

- Does it supply at least some of what each person needs? Review that list of priorities you made before you had a definite trip in mind. Does this trip fit the bill?
- Does it respect what various family members can't do? Consider this trip in terms of the ages, capabilities, and limitations of both you and your children.
- What about the pace of the trip? Think carefully about what you plan to do. Are you covering an unrealistic amount of territory, or planning for too much activity? Or will you be bored or disappointed at what you've missed because the pace is too slow?
- How much will the trip change your family's normal routine? Any differences in scenery and culture or pace and style should suit your family's needs right now. Greater changes may require a longer adjustment period. How long a vacation do you have, and how quickly can you all adapt?

Obviously, all of these are questions of balance. At this stage of the planning, just asking them is enough; you will be able to sense whether the answers feel right. As you check your trip against such variables, you can adapt it to reduce the physical and psychological stresses you are likely to encounter.

Last of all, ask yourselves whether the trip's potential for success depends on everything going just right. If the ingredients aren't all perfect, will the vacation be a disaster? Is there room for flexibility?

You must expect to be flexible when you travel. There will be moments when your best-laid plans just won't pan out; the plane will be late, the weather rainy, or the restaurant dinner too long for your two-year-old. No matter how carefully you plan, some changes may be needed along the way. Still, your considered and orderly planning of your trip will surely have reduced the potential for chaos; and, more important, you will have increased the chances that the whole family will have a really good time.

Designing Your Trip

Now that you've decided where and how to go, it's time to nail down the details of your trip. Make the broad decisions months before departure; you can deal with the smaller details as you get closer to departure day.

Make the basic arrangements. For now, make the arrangements that form the skeleton of the trip and are not likely to change. Reserve your places for any package deal or tour you want. Make your plane or long-distance train reservations. Arrange to rent a car, keeping in mind when and where you can pick it up and drop it off. Reserve your rooms at the resort or hotel where you plan to stay awhile, or make a deposit toward your house or apartment rental. If you're going on a camping trip, reserve your campsite now. If you will be staying in various places and want to leave some flexibility in the schedule, at least reserve your accommodations for the first and last nights; you won't want to hunt for a room just after or just before a tiring journey. All of these arrangements should be made as far ahead as possible. If you are traveling to Europe in the summer, the longer you wait the less selection you will have, and the same is true of warm-weather destinations during midwinter school vacation weeks and of popular tourist areas at any time of year.

Now that you've committed yourselves to a basic trip plan, you can spend the next several months reading and talking about

---

A magazine article sent us on one of our most memorable travel adventures. We had both been great fans of "The Prisoner," an offbeat spy series that was on TV during the 1960s. It took place in a village, ostensibly on a remote island in an unnamed part of the world. The village itself was the most surrealistic collection of bizarre architectural structures one could concoct. Imagine our surprise when we stumbled on this article, which told us that the village really exists and is, in fact, part of a hotel complex just outside the town of Porthmadog in north-central Wales. We stayed at the hotel, roaming the winding alleys of the village and playing at being spies. We loved it, and so did the kids. How often does one get to act out one's favorite fantasies?

---

the places you'll be going and dreaming about what you'll do there. To get started, you'll want to collect travel literature and maps.

Gather specific information about the places you will visit. Remember those newspaper and magazine articles you clipped and saved when you were gathering ideas? Take out the pertinent ones and remind yourself about those events or sights that you want to be sure to catch, or certain lodgings or restaurants that interest you. Go back to the bookstore and invest in a guidebook or two suitable to your needs. Check with the airlines for pamphlets or brochures. To promote tourism in their countries, foreign airlines in particular often offer extensive travel literature, including helpful pamphlets about customs requirements, climate, staying healthy, currency exchange, shopping, metric conversions, and more.

You'll also want to write to the tourist offices of the cities and states or countries you will visit; ask for information pertaining to your particular trip. Tell them when you will be there, for how long, and what you want to see and do. The more specific your requests are, the more they will be able to assist you. Here are some suggestions:

- If you're still looking for places to stay, tell them what kinds of accommodations interest you (hotels, guesthouses, campgrounds) or ask what variety is available; some unusual lodgings, like farms or castles, may delight your kids.
- Tell them what your price range is, and ask whether they have a list of accommodations with ratings.
- Ask about native foods. You may receive descriptions of some of the traditional specialties, or even, as in the "Taste of Scotland" program, a directory of eating establishments that offer them.
- Ask for whatever maps you'll need—road maps if you are driving, or public transit maps and schedules if you're not. Many cities offer tourist maps, which show the major streets and arteries and important sites.
- Ask for calendars of special events that will be taking place during your stay—concerts, opera, ballet, museum exhibitions, and festivals.

As you collect information, share it with the children; this can make for lovely dinner conversation for months before a big trip (for children especially, anticipation is a big part of the fun). As you discuss what you will do and see, you will begin to get a greater feel for the places you're going, and eventually figure out how to fill in your itinerary.

> *It's easy to make grand promises to the kids, to get them excited and involved in the trip's planning. But don't talk about things you may not end up doing; if you do you'll regret it later, especially if your children are young.*

Obtain travel documents. If you will be leaving the United States, several months before your departure you will need to begin work on obtaining certain documents.

Passports. If you will travel only within the United States or to Canada, Mexico, or one of certain other countries and territories, you do not need passports. You may still need proof of U.S. citizenship, such as a birth certificate or voter registration card. For most trips abroad, though, passports are necessary; check with the consulates of the countries you plan to visit, a U.S. passport agency, or a travel agent to be sure (see the Appendix). Apply for passports as soon as you know you will need them, preferably several months in advance (earlier if you also need visas). Getting passports takes longer during the spring and summer, when most applications are made.

> *Each member of the family—including your infant—needs his or her own passport. It used to be that minor children could be included on the passport of a parent, but no more. As of this writing, passports for children under eighteen are good for five years and cost $40. For adults the fee is $65, and the validity period is ten years. Passport applications are available from U.S. passport agencies (see the Appendix), from some post offices, and from federal and state courthouses.*

Visas. A stamp placed in your passport by the government of a foreign country, a visa authorizes you to visit that country for a stated purpose (tourism is one). Not all countries require visas;

most Western European countries simply stamp your passport upon arrival. But it is wise to check whether the countries on your itinerary require you to apply in advance. When you go to the passport agency to obtain your passport (which you must do first, since you need to have a passport to apply for a visa), you can ask for the pamphlet *Foreign Entry Requirements*. Updated annually, it will tell you where and how to apply for visas. But requirements may change between editions, so it is best to double-check with the embassy or consulate of the country in question. You can find the addresses of embassies and consulates in *The Congressional Directory*, available in most libraries, and in the telephone directories of many large U.S. cities (foreign consulates are heavily concentrated in Chicago, New Orleans, New York, San Francisco, and Washington, DC). A good travel agent or an airline serving your country of destination should also be able to give you the latest information on visa requirements.

Getting visas may take several weeks, so apply early, particularly if you need visas for more than one country (since the issuing agency needs your passports, you can apply to only one country at a time). Visas vary in how long they are valid and whether they are renewable. Be sure your visas won't expire before you even arrive!

Immunizations. Some countries you visit may require you to carry an international certificate of vaccination, showing that you have been immunized against certain diseases. These requirements can change suddenly. To find out whether you will need shots, contact the U.S. Public Health Service, your local or state health department, or the embassy or consulate of each country you plan to visit. It may also be wise to ask your physician and the kids' whether they recommend vaccinations that may not be required. Do all this early; if you are going to need more than one shot, you'll want time to space them out as needed.

International driver's permit. Many countries require this permit for visitors who drive during their stay. Canada and Mexico do not require the permit. Your auto club can tell you whether you'll need a permit and, if so, issue it to you; this takes several weeks.

Insurance. Ask your insurance agent whether your homeowner's insurance covers lost or stolen baggage while you are away from home. Likewise, find out if your medical insurance will cover expenses incurred on your trip, particularly if you are going out of the United States. If you have adequate coverage, find out the best procedure for filing claims (do you pay the provider and then get reimbursed, or do you take claim forms along?) and what information the insurance company will want should you get medical services while away. If you do not have adequate insurance coverage, talk to your agent about getting a policy to cover the trip, or ask a travel agent about travel insurance.

Fill in your itinerary. Now that you've read and discussed the information you gathered about your destination, it's time to figure out what you want to do when. If making the basic reservations provided the skeleton of your trip, then developing an itinerary will put meat on the bones.

For a simple trip—a week at the beach, or a visit to relatives in the Midwest—just a list of things of interest in the area will do. Note which attractions or activities are available only at certain times or on certain days. Once your arrive, you can use this list to choose what you'd like to do each day.

For a touring trip, your task is somewhat more complicated. Whether you're going by car, recreational vehicle, train, or bus, get out a map of the area you will be covering. Decide where you want to go and what you want to see, and the best order in which to do things. Try to plan a schedule of when you'll go from place to place and how long you'll stay at each one.

A sound touring itinerary for the family will enable you to see and do an enjoyable amount without causing death or divorce in the process. Don't overdo the distances that you'll cover each day; twelve hours in a car or on a bus will leave you all bleary-eyed and in no mood to enjoy anything. Break up the distances into stretches well within everyone's tolerance. Next, think realistically about how much you can see and do in the time you have available. Most of us tend to pack too much into one trip, so try to weed out things that are less important to you. Finally, intersperse quiet days, or at least days when the pace will be slower, among the days of heavier activity. In the midst of a week of sightseeing, spending a day lounging around the hotel pool can have wondrous restorative powers.

Your itinerary should not be etched in stone; it is a guideline to be altered as need be. Expect to make changes in it as you continue reading and talking about your trip, and, once the trip is underway, don't feel you have to do everything according to schedule. If little Sarah gets carsick and you get behind on your driving, you can make up for lost time another day, or just skip a sight or two.

Make other advance preparations. There are some other preparations that you may want to make a month or two before your trip.

First, will you want someone to watch your house? You may feel more comfortable having a house sitter actually living on the premises, especially if you'll be away several weeks or longer. College students are sometimes available for such duties; you may be able to find one through the school housing office or by posting a notice wherever advertisements for student jobs are displayed on campus. Or you may have friends who would enjoy a change of scene by staying at your place for a while. You can also find house sitters through newspaper ads. With any stranger, of course, be sure to check references.

If you don't feel you need a house sitter, you'll probably still want to ask a neighbor to keep a casual eye on things. Let your neighbor know the dates you will be away, what lights you will leave on and whether they are on timers, and so on. This will help your neighbor notice anything that looks suspicious while you're away.

If you have animals, you will need to think about their care. Likewise, you may need someone to look after your indoor plants and your garden, especially if you will be gone for a long time. With a house sitter these matters can easily be worked into the arrangement; otherwise you will need the services of a friend, neighbor, or kennel. Your family might arrange with another to care for each other's pets and plants when either of you travel. Or you might hire a teenage neighbor to feed the animals and water plants.

If you're going away for a long time or to an exotic place, it will be wise to arrange medical and dental checkups for each member of the family before you go. We'll discuss medical preparations in more detail in a later chapter.

Final Arrangements

Let's say that it's now several weeks to a month before your departure. You have made major reservations, worked on your itinerary, and arranged for travel documents and care of the homestead while you are gone. There are a few more specific decisions to make that will help to ensure a smoother trip.

Make reservations. If you are going to be traveling from place to place, you should make reservations now for accommodations where you definitely want to stay, particularly if you're going to a popular destination or traveling during the tourist season. You may also want to reserve rooms if you are likely to arrive late in the day. To go scouting about for room at the inn when you're all exhausted is a good way to arouse crankiness in everybody. Also, if certain accommodations have something special to offer the kids, you might want to book now just to make sure you'll get in. Don't feel you have to make reservations for each night on the road, though; you'll want to allow for flexibility in your schedule.

When traveling in cold weather, we look first for hotels with indoor heated pools and reserve ahead because this feature adds so much to the kids' pleasure in staying overnight.

For those days when it seems just as well not to reserve ahead, it helps to have a few possible accommodations in mind in case you end up arriving late or tired. This may save you from frantically searching through books and brochures as you are driving into town.

Do your shopping. Figure out what things you'll need to buy for your trip. Consider climate conditions as well as the kind of activities you have planned. Is everyone equipped with a bathing suit, hiking boots, sun hat? In addition, think about the kinds of books, toys, or games you will want to have for the kids on the plane, in the car, or in hotels and restaurants. And how about the conveniences that make travel so much more relaxing—a Thermos for cold drinks in the car, a picnic hamper? See chapters 4 and 5 for advice on what to take, and shop now for those items you don't already have.

See to last-minute details. You have a week or so to go. Time to get things in order so that you will be ready to leave with an easy mind and a holiday spirit.

- Buy travelers' checks if you plan to use them. Most travelers do, rather than carrying large amounts of cash or relying solely on credit cards. Auto clubs often offer travelers' checks free or at discounts for members; so do some savings and loan associations for their account holders. But where you should get your travelers' checks may depend on what company's checks are offered. Find out which travelers' check companies have the most convenient network of offices where you will be, and what services they will make available to you. For instance, can you cash a personal check should you run into some difficulty? What procedures must you go through to replace lost or stolen checks? If you are to be away for a lengthy period, ask whether the company will receive mail for its customers.

When you buy travelers' checks get a mix of denominations; this way you won't have to sign several checks every time you pay a hotel or restaurant bill, or pay for a newspaper with a check for one hundred dollars. We get most of our checks in hundred- and fifty-dollar denominations, which we use to pay large bills and to cash as we go along so we have some currency in our pockets. We also get a smaller quantity in twenties for those occasions when we want to have just a little extra cash.

- If you are going abroad, consider obtaining a small amount of the currency for the countries you will visit; some banks and travel agents sell foreign currency starter packets. Changing currency here may not always get you the best exchange rate, but having a small amount on hand when you arrive is convenient for tipping, paying the fare from airport to hotel, and so on. This way changing currency is one less thing you have to do the minute you arrive. Do check whether the governments in question impose restrictions on bringing in their currency from outside the country.
- Pay any bills that will come due while you are away.
- Arrange with the post office to hold your mail during your trip, or arrange with a neighbor or friend to collect it daily from your mailbox. Make similar arrangements regarding your daily newspaper. Mail piling up in a box or a stack of papers on the front lawn is tantamount to posting a sign on the house announcing your absence.
- If you plan to leave timers attached to lights to make the

house look occupied, make sure that the timers are in working order.
- Complete your arrangements for caretaking of house, pets, and plants. Give your house key to the house sitter or neighbor. Write up the instructions you want to leave. Make sure that you have sufficient supplies of pet food on hand. If a neighbor is keeping an eye on the house, let him or her know where and when timed lights should go on.
- Give a copy of your itinerary along with the names and addresses of some places where you can be reached to the person looking out for your house, so that you can be contacted in an emergency. It's a good idea to give the same information to a family member, in case you need to be reached in some family crisis. Also leave a list of the serial numbers of your travelers' checks with a trusted person, in case you lose both your checks and the separate list of serial numbers that you should be carrying with you.
- Finish your shopping. Don't leave it until the last couple of days if you don't want to leave in a frenzy.
- Put your jewelry, bank books, credit cards that you won't be taking, and other valuables in a safe place such as a bank's safe-deposit box.
- Start packing. You will still be at it on the last day, but an early start makes packing a much calmer task.
- If a friend or relative is to drive you to the airport or train station, or pick you up upon your return, call to confirm the date and time. Make sure to supply all the pertinent information (flight number, date and time) that your friend or relative will need to meet you when you get back.

The Day of Departure

At last! The adrenaline is flowing, and you're almost ready to go. Here is a list of things to do before you leave the house.

- Make sure that you have with you and readily accessible all your necessary papers—passports, visas, plane or train tickets, vaccination certificates, international driver's permit, confirmation of reservations, insurance forms, credit cards, and travelers' checks.
- Connect the timers to the lights, and set them.

A PLANNING CHECKLIST

4 to 5 Months Ahead

___ Make plane or train reservations
___ Reserve rental car
___ Reserve main accommodations
___ Make tour reservations
___ Collect travel literature

2 to 3 Months Ahead

___ Get passports
___ Get visas
___ Get immunizations
___ Get international driver's permit

1 to 2 Months Ahead

___ Search for housesitter
___ Plan itinerary
___ Get health checkups
   ___ Doctor
   ___ Dentist
   ___ Prescriptions current?
   ___ Special prescriptions?
___ Check insurance coverage
   ___ Medical
   ___ Homeowners'
   ___ Travel
___ Make any other necessary accommodations reservations

2 to 4 Weeks Ahead

___ Do shopping
   ___ Clothes
   ___ Toys
   ___ Books
   ___ Food
   ___ Equipment
___ Arrange for pet and plant care
___ Arrange ride to airport or station

One Week Ahead

___ Get travelers' checks
___ Get foreign currencies (starter amounts)
___ Have mail held or picked up
___ Pay bills due during vacation
___ Check light timers
___ Write instructions for house and pet caretaker
___ Give keys to caretaker
___ Give itinerary to caretaker and family members
___ List serial numbers of travelers' checks (give one copy to caretaker or family member)
___ Put valuables in safekeeping
___ Stop newspaper or have it picked up
___ Begin packing
___ Confirm ride to airport or station

A PLANNING CHECKLIST (*continued*)

Day of Departure

Documents to take
- ___ Passports
- ___ Visas
- ___ ID documents
- ___ Plane or train tickets
- ___ Other transportation tickets
- ___ Rental car papers
- ___ International driver's permit
- ___ Accommodations confirmations
- ___ Tour vouchers
- ___ Credit cards
- ___ Travelers' checks
- ___ Serial numbers of travelers' checks (carried separately)
- ___ Foreign currencies
- ___ Vaccination certificates
- ___ Prescriptions
- ___ Number to call if credit cards lost or stolen
- ___ Insurance forms

Household
- ___ Connect and set timers
- ___ Unplug appliances
- ___ Turn refrigerator to lowest setting and discard perishable foods
- ___ Wash dishes
- ___ Run garbage disposal
- ___ Empty trash
- ___ Turn off furnace and water heater (in warm weather)
- ___ Turn down thermostat (in cold weather)
- ___ Close fireplace flu
- ___ Turn off faucets (including washing machine)
- ___ Unplug sinks
- ___ Flush toilets
- ___ Lock doors and windows

- Unplug appliances and lamps that will not be in use while you are away (not the refrigerator, though—just turn it to its lowest setting).
- Take out the trash, and make sure there is no food left sitting in the garbage disposal.
- In warm weather, if no one is staying in your house, turn off the water heater and furnace. In cold weather, turn the thermostat down.
- Make sure all doors and windows are locked and the fireplace flue is closed.
- Check to see that all faucets are turned off tightly, including those connected to the washing machine. Leave the sinks unstopped.
- If you have small children, make sure that everyone has finished with last-minute toileting and all the toilets have been flushed.

Now you're ready. We can't guarantee that you won't have overlooked something or that your vacation will be glorious because of the way you planned it, but if you have gone through the stages of planning and preparation in a thoughtful and orderly way, you've certainly increased the chances that everyone will have a happy and memorable trip. Bon voyage!

CHAPTER FOUR
Planes, Trains, Cars, and RVs

THE TRIP FROM HOME to vacation spot can be as simple as an hour's drive to the beach cottage or as involved as a day-long flight complete with layovers and plane changes. For an ambitious trip, how to get to your destination can be one of the most important decisions you will make about your vacation. This journey can also represent one of the most expensive items in the travel budget. Yet transportation decisions sometimes seem like a spider's web of fares, schedules, and competing claims. Should we fly? With what airline? Is train travel still an effective way to get around? Will I really save money by driving?

In this chapter, we'll attempt to sort through the maze. We'll examine most of the major means of getting you from point A to point B, raise pertinent questions, and look at the choices you have, so that when the time comes you will be able to select the best combination of arrangements for your family. In Chapter 6, we'll discuss how to make transportation by each of these means a more relaxed and enjoyable experience.

Going by Air

The reason for choosing to fly is usually simple: Either the distance demands it, or speed in getting there is important. Certainly the flight experience can be exciting and adventurous for children, but few parents would spring for the cost of air fares for the whole family for that reason alone. High cost is the major disadvantage of flying; the frenetic aspects of airports and plane schedules is another. If you are well informed, you can reduce the cost of air travel and make it more enjoyable. Shop around, asking a lot of questions. This will take time, and you may feel as if you are making a nuisance of yourself, but you may well be rewarded with the most comfortable flight at the lowest possible cost. What are the factors to consider?

Which airlines fly to your destination? If you have been reading travel literature and looking at newspaper and magazine ads, you may already have some names in mind. Otherwise, if you'll be leaving the United States you can start with the national airline of the country you are heading for; a travel agent should be able to suggest a few other airlines that serve your destination. Finally, call a few of the large airlines (toll-free numbers are listed in the yellow pages) and ask if they fly to where you want to go. They will also give you information about their competitors if you ask, but keep in mind that it may not be complete and up to date.

Will you have to make stops? A *nonstop* flight will usually be the simplest and fastest way to your destination. A *direct* flight means that you won't have to change planes, but you may make one or more stops to discharge and pick up passengers. Whether you stay on board or spend forty-five minutes in the terminal, each stop adds yet another period in which you'll have to keep your young ones occupied.

If your flight is not described as nonstop or direct, you may be in for that old bugaboo, a *connecting* flight. Sometimes this can't be avoided, particularly when small, regional airports or international destinations are involved, but if you are offered a multiplane routing do make sure it can't be done more simply.

Connecting flights are more of a hassle if you are switching airlines; at some big airports, this means moving to a different terminal. In any event, you must allow enough time to make the connection in a reasonably sane manner. This is one area in which booking agents sometimes aren't careful enough; the time required for making connections can vary quite a bit at different airports. When you make reservations, ask how long getting from one gate to another should take. Depending on the length of your kids' legs and the impediment of your carry-on luggage, you may want an extra fifteen to twenty minutes' allowance between flights.

What seats should you choose? Choose the arrangement that seems best suited to your family: the four or five across in the center section of a "widebody" plane, or seats across the aisle from each other, or some of you behind the others if you prefer to separate the children. On an uncrowded flight, your booking agent may do you an especially good turn and spread your seats across a long row with empty seats in between to spread out in.

If you hope the kids will nap during the flight, choose seats away from galleys and lavatories. If your child will need to get up and stretch frequently or pay a few visits to the restroom, an aisle seat will help.

On flights abroad where smoking is permitted, the air will seem fresher at least five rows in front of the smoking section.

The bulkhead seats—the first row of seats in the cabin—are sometimes more comfortable for traveling families. Since there are no seats in front of these, there is a bit more space for wiggling feet; this also means, however, that there is no convenient place to stow carry-on bags. You will probably have several such bags among you, and you are not permitted to leave them lying about; you can store them in the overhead compartments, but you'll have to get up to fetch them when you need them.

Choose your seats as early as possible; you may be able to do so when you make reservations.

Is there a choice of airports? This is one question that most people never think to ask; yet it can be quite important in choosing a flight. Let's say you want to fly to Washington, DC, or New York City. Each city is served by three airports; where will your flight land? A choice of airports is possible with many overseas trips, too; most flights from the United States to England, for example, land at Heathrow Airport, but some disembark at Gatwick. To decide if it makes a difference to you, you will want to know how close your first night's accommodations are to each airport, what ground transportation is available at each, and at what cost. Ask about airport buses, hotel or other limousines, public transportation, taxis, or car rental agencies.

What kinds of amenities does the airline offer? All the customary "extras" that go with a flight—meals, snacks, entertainment, and the like—can take on extra importance when you must keep kids occupied and contented, and the longer the flight the more attention you should pay to the extras. The low-cost, no-frills airlines usually don't include such conveniences in the price of the ticket, but most people use the more traditional airlines; if the fares are equal or nearly so, then the amenities offered should become more important in your choice.

When making your inquiries about flights, ask whether a meal will be served. All other things being equal, choose a flight with food. The kids will enjoy being served their own trays and opening all the cute little containers on the little foldout tables, even if they won't eat the food.

Most airlines have menus available to serve different needs (kosher, vegetarian, low-calorie, and so forth), and for our purposes the most important is the children's menu. Some airlines change the children's menu every few weeks; others offer a choice among several alternatives, such as hot dog, hamburger, fried chicken, spaghetti, and the classic peanut-butter-and-jelly sandwich.

Some airlines offer a free baby meal: an infant cup and spoon, napkins, cereal, a half-pint of milk, and jars of strained or mashed meat, vegetables, and fruit. Others stock some baby food on board in case families forget to bring some; the airlines don't advertise this, though, and you should not assume they will have baby food available.

Inquire about food for children and infants early. When you make your reservations, tell the airline what you would like. You may be able to reserve special meals as late as twenty-four hours ahead. If you reserve your special meals further in advance, call the day before departure to confirm that you'll get them.

Many airlines make infant bassinets available at no charge. These differ somewhat in size and type. One major airline has a disposable bassinet that you put on the floor in front of you (you have to sit in the bulkhead seats to use it); another carries one that fits on the bulkhead seats, fastened in place with a seatbelt;

another uses a type that hangs anchored to attachments on the cabin walls. Sizes vary from 23 inches to 31 inches, so if you want a bassinet make sure that your baby will fit into it. There are obviously limits on the number of bassinets that can be used on a single flight, since the number of bulkhead seats and special attachments is limited; so be sure to reserve yours as early as the airline will permit. Without a bassinet, you'll have to keep your baby on your laps throughout the flight.

Many airlines carry a variety of other infant paraphernalia, especially on long flights. These may include items such as disposable diapers, bottles, creams and powders, and bibs. You might ask the airline for a list of these, as well as for any pamphlet they might have on traveling with infants or older children.

If your baby has a cold when you're planning to fly, you may want to give her some decongestant at least an hour before takeoff. Otherwise her eustachian tubes may become painfully backed up during takeoff.
Whether your baby is sick or not, nurse her, or give her a bottle, during takeoff and landing. Her swallowing will relieve the discomfort of air pressure changes.

Flights longer than three hours or so usually offer movies. There are always seats from which you cannot see the movie, so ask about that when choosing your seats.

What types of fares can you choose from? We've saved the best for last. Welcome to the jungle! Airfare plans and terminology can be confusing, but we shall present the most important features of the current major fare types as simply as we can.

Passengers flying *first class* receive a bit more attention, more leg and elbow room, and some extra amenities; they pay anywhere from 20 percent to 60 percent more than the full coach fare for the same flight.

Coach, or *economy*, class is where everyone else sits; and here an amazing phenomenon of air travel can be observed. If you sit in the coach section, you and your fellow passengers will sit in the same size seats, receive exactly the same service, and arrive at the same place at the same time—but you will have paid enormously different amounts. This occurs because of all the discounted fares and promotional programs offered in this highly competitive industry.

Never be satisfied merely to be quoted coach or economy fare; while not as much as first class, full coach fare is the most expensive tariff you can pay to fly in a coach seat. You want to know instead what *discount* fares are available; those are the ones you've seen in the advertisements. Each flight has a certain number of seats set aside for discount fares. The object of the airline is to fill as many seats as possible; there will be more discounted seats available on the more lightly traveled flights. (If you're going to Florida during Christmas week, you had better reserve way, way ahead of time if you hope to fly for less.)

Discount fares are figured as a percentage of full coach fare. There are several different types of discount fares; the major ones are as follows.

Off-peak fares. These can be 20 to 25 percent cheaper than regular coach fares, with no restrictions. They are offered at slow travel times, like late at night or very early in the morning, or on a slow day of the week for a given route.

Excursion fares. The rules for these vary, but generally you must purchase a round-trip ticket and return within a specified time period. Typical are those that require you to stay longer than 7 but no more than 21 days; 14 to 45 days is another popular variation. You do not necessarily need to reserve far ahead to obtain excursion fares, but at heavy travel times some airlines may limit the numbers of excursion seats. Excursion fares may be slightly more expensive if you depart or return on a weekend.

APEX fares. The Advance Purchase Excursion fare is for travel between the United States and a foreign country. As with the excursion fare, your return must fall within a certain number of days (usually 14 to 45) from your departure. But unlike simple excursion fares, APEX fares must be reserved and paid in advance. How far ahead you must do so varies with each airline. Some carriers have a Super APEX fare, which is even cheaper but carries different restrictions. Again, ask.

Bargain fares. This general category of fares is ordinarily for domestic travel only, and goes under different names at different airlines. You must reserve and pay for your tickets some specified number of days in advance. Some deals may require you to stay a minimum number of days before you return. Once again, different rules apply with different carriers.

Promotional fares. These are the cutthroat fares of the airline industry. The ads offering "coast to coast for $99 each way," or "kids fly free" come under this category; they are sales promotions developed to stimulate business during a slow time or to take business from the competition on a particular route. Such fares change all the time and are heavily advertised. Don't, by the way, call a reservations agent and ask if the airline has any "promotional fares." You will need to ask for a specific fare program that you've seen advertised.

Although bargain and promotional fares can be great deals, they may have strings attached. They most often require nonrefundable advance payment. You may even have to pay a penalty to make a change in your flight schedule. Should you have to forfeit your payment, though, some airlines will credit the amount toward future travel. And it may be possible to obtain a refund in the event of illness if you have a note from a doctor.

Children's fares. These are the prices charged for children flying with an adult. Even discounted fares are sometimes discounted further for children, although those very cheap promotional fares (referred to in the industry as "deep discounts") are usually the same for everyone, regardless of age. Some general rules apply to children's fares, though these rules may vary depending on the airline, destination, and season.

- Children under two years of age fly free on domestic routes; they are assigned no seats but are expected to sit in a parent's lap.
- For foreign travel, children under two pay 10 percent of the adult fare.
- Within the United States, kids ages two through eleven usually pay 75 percent of adult fare, though this can drop to as low as 50 percent, and the age range may be extended to as high as seventeen.
- Children two through eleven usually pay 50 to 75 percent of the full adult fare (or, perhaps, of the adult excursion fare) to foreign destinations.

It is not always necessary for children to fly in the same fare category as the adults they are traveling with. Since the price of a child's ticket is calculated differently in different fare categories, it may be cheaper for the kids to fly in one fare category while you use another. For example, you may want to buy a child's seven- to fourteen-day excursion ticket along with some other bargain tickets for you and your spouse. When shopping for tickets, then, ask for the adult rates and the children's rates for each type of fare available, and put together the least expensive combination you can.

Don't be confused by the dizzying array of catchy names that airlines use for their fares. So long as you can explain what you are looking for, airline representatives will help you track down what's available. But let's quickly summarize some general principles of inexpensive air travel. It's usually cheaper to fly—

- during the week rather than on weekends (though this is not always true for bargain and promotional fares);
- at night or early in the morning;
- when you stay longer;
- when you reserve and pay for your tickets well in advance;
- when you travel at slower times of the year (during the off-season or "shoulder season").

It is often possible to obtain discount fares even if you fly to your destination with one carrier and return with another, although some fares require you to fly both ways with the same airline.

It is usually a good idea to pay for your fare ahead of time. Under the "guaranteed fare policy" adopted by the airline industry, once you have paid for your tickets you are protected from increases in fares, other charges, or changes in rules that take place before your trip. This policy may not apply to some overseas flights, but it is almost always upheld for domestic flights. If you have paid ahead and the fares go down, many airlines will rewrite your ticket at the lower cost—*if* you ask them to (no reservations agent will call you to say, "Hey, the price just went down!").

When making your reservations you want to find out—

- if there are any restrictions attached to your fare, and, if so, what they are;
- if there are penalties should you cancel or change plans (for instance, you might lose your discount or be charged a fixed fee if you change flights with insufficient notice);
- how long in advance you must pay to guarantee the low-cost fare.

If you are paying for and receiving your tickets by mail, you must send your payment early enough to ensure that it will reach the airline by the specified deadline. It is safer to charge airline fares to a credit card, so your payment can be confirmed on the spot.

What about air charters and tour packages? Signing up for a chartered flight or package tour can be a good alternative to booking a flight through a commercial airline. In the case of the air charter, an airline sells a block of tickets to a wholesale travel agency or charter company; that company, in turn, sells them to the public either directly or through another retail travel agency. If you can find a charter flight that fits your needs, it may be the cheapest way to go. You will probably have less choice with a charter deal, however; you may have fewer departurer dates to choose from, and your return date may be automatically determined by the departure date you select. With charter flights, too, there are almost invariably pay-ahead requirements, various restrictions, and cancellation penalties.

Some of the warnings you may have heard about chartered flights are worth heeding. Travelers are sometimes left stranded when charter flights fail to happen, and departure times are sometimes changed at the last minute—a nightmare particularly if you are waiting in the airport with small children for a midnight flight to London. The best way to avoid such an experience is to be confident of the travel agency with which you are dealing, and to satisfy yourself that the wholesale charter company supplying the tickets has a good track record.

Be aware that seats may be closer together on very long flights or those offering bargain rates.

Tour packages, which combine air travel with such services as hotel accommodations and car rentals, can be obtained from airlines, travel agencies, and companies like American Express, Thomas Cook, and the American Automobile Association. If such a package tour suits you, it may be a welcome way to go. It's possible to save enough on the airfare to make such a plan economical even if you don't use all the other services.

However you book your flight, it's a good idea to call back a week or so later to confirm the reservations, the flight information, and the fare. Then, about a week before departure, recheck the flight information one more time (once in a while departure and landing schedules change) and make sure that the airline has reserved any special items you requested, such as children's meals or a bassinet. If you have been allowed to choose your seats in advance, confirm your seat selection as well.

Going by Train

In these days of jet airliners and high-speed highways reaching into all corners of the landscape, the train has fallen in the eyes of many American families into a lowered position on the list of options. Ought it to be on yours? Think about what it offers, pro and con.

The romance of train travel may not be what it was in the heyday of the railroads, when luxury liners were hailed as "cruiseships on wheels." Yet in recent years Amtrak has attempted to revive this image; today's Superliners feature lounges and multilevel observation cars with wraparound windows. Overseas, rail travel is often comfortable and efficient, from the restored splendor (and sky-high fares) of the Orient Express to the more mundane but highly serviceable intercity rail connections throughout Europe. Going by train can be a way to view the scenery without the fatigue of driving or the worry about car trouble in strange places. And it can be a wonderful way to meet new people from all over the world.

Although trains can't match the speed of airplanes (it can take as much as a full day to ride by rail from the Eastern seaboard to Chicago), they can be fine for shorter trips or for destination hopping, such as when you're visiting a group of countries in Europe.

As for spontaneous side trips, the train offers less flexibility than the car but more than the plane. You pay for the privilege, of course—more about that when we discuss fares.

Finally, going by train is not always cheap. In this country, the expense can often approach or equal that of flying. For a long trip, sleeping accommodations and meals must be added to the basic fare. Some discount family or excursion packages are available, as with air travel; and in some foreign places, where gas and airfares are very expensive, taking the train can be a real bargain.

U.S. train travel. Compared with making your way through the airline jungle, getting information about domestic train service is fairly simple. There is only one source to contact: Amtrak, the nation's rail passenger system. If you are considering making train travel a part of your trip, call or write the nearest Amtrak office and ask for a copy of the *National Train Timetables*. This booklet not only lists routes and schedules but also tells what services are available on different trains and lists many connecting bus services. Ask in addition for Amtrak's *Travel Planner*, a brochure describing the type of trains used on different routes, including eating and sleeping arrangements. It also includes information about hotel, tour, car rental, and air packages. These publications will help you decide whether train travel will fit your plans, and provide you with the information you need to make further inquiries. Amtrak also has pamphlets about some particular routes.

Armed with all this information, you should be able to figure out whether you can get where you want to go by train and, if so, how long it will take. It's always wise to double-check by calling Amtrak to confirm that the printed information is still correct. Also make sure that you know all the options available on your route, and check the costs. Be sure to check where and how often you will have to change trains or lay over.

The reason for all of this double checking is that the variety of trains and services on board is immense. The trains vary from the standard cars used in short to medium routes, with fewer amenities and more frequent stops, to faster trains, such as the Turboliners and high-speed Metroliners, which are used on only a few routes, including the Northeast corridor. There are also trains designed for longer journeys; the sleek, modern Superliners now in use on long-distance routes offer the latest in Amtrak luxuries, including various bedroom–sitting room combinations. Amtrak continues to add new car configurations, so always ask what's available.

When it comes to the amenities offered during the trip, you can run into a problem unique to train travel: The amenities may be available during only part of your trip. For instance, the booklet may say that your train has a dining car, but the dining car may be added or disconnected at some point along the way. Or the booklet may tell you that baggage checking is available on a given train. But not all stations are equipped to provide this service; if your departure or destination station is not, you cannot use the service. Although all of this information is listed in the *National Train Timetables*, it's wise to ask in case you missed something. You'll want to know—

Will you be able to check your baggage through? If you can check your luggage when you depart and pick it up at your destination, you've got the same easy arrangement as with an airline; you've only your carry-ons to deal with. Remember, baggage-checking service must be available at both your start and end points for it to be of use to you.

What food services will there be? There is a wide variety; check to see which will be available on your train.

- *When there is no dining car.* Meal services go by many names, which differ depending on the train. There are cafes, buffets, dinettes, and lounge cars; you may be offered hot and cold sandwiches, snacks, or tray meals. There may be tables to eat at, or you may carry your food back to your seat. You'll want to ask what kinds of foods and dining areas are available on the train you are considering.
- *Complete dining and beverage service.* This is how Cary Grant and James Bond always eat on trains in the movies, seated in a dining car that has waiters and white tablecloths. Complete meals are provided, at restaurant prices.
- *Club car service.* If you have arranged for first-class reserved seating, an attendant will take your order and deliver a tray to your seat. You eat on a little lap table; both the food and style of service are comparable to that on airplanes.

Must you reserve in advance? Some trains are referred to as "all-reserved"; on these, all seats are booked in advance. These are generally long-distance trains or premium trains such as Metroliners and Superliners. Find out how far in advance you should book.

What sleeping accommodations are available? Beds or berths will add a hefty amount to the cost of your train trip, but on an overnight journey you may feel that they are worth the extra cost. Again, there are variations.

- *Sleeping car.* In this first-class sleeper you can get a compartment that sleeps one (called a roomette) or one that sleeps two (called a bedroom). Your compartment will have a thermostat, a sink, a mirror, a closet, and a toilet (in its own separate room if you reserve a bedroom). You may even choose a bedroom suite—two adjoining bedrooms with the dividing partition removed.

The choices are different aboard the luxurious Superliners. The "family bedroom" sleeps four and has a toilet down the hall. The "economy bedroom," designed for one or two passengers, converts reclining seats into beds. The "deluxe bedroom" gives you a private toilet and shower, a picture window, and more room than the others. Two adjoining deluxe bedrooms can be combined to become a four-person suite.

- *Slumber coach.* This is the economy-class sleeper of the industry. You can get a single or a double with the same features as in the sleeping car, but the compartment will be smaller, the berths smaller, the mattresses thinner, and the toilet always in the main compartment.

The costs of these various options vary considerably, so check carefully. It's also advisable, especially when traveling with larger children, to check on the berth or bed dimensions. You want to choose accommodations that don't require any family members to become accordions at night.

What types of fares are available? Coach seats on the unreserved trains are the least expensive. Club car seating, sleeping accommodations, and all Metroliner seats are more costly and must be reserved in advance. Some discount plans are available, as follows.

- *Children's fares.* The standard fare for a child two to fifteen is half of the adult fare. For each adult traveler you may take two children under the age of two for no cost; they will be expected to share your seat.

- *Promotional fares.* Amtrak advertises special deals from time to time. For instance, one such program divides the country into three regions, then, for a highly discounted fare, allows for three planned stops within a region during a 45-day period. A surcharge is added to cross into another region, but the savings are still substantial.

- *Excursions.* As with some of the airlines' excursion fares, you must go and return within a specified period of time. Advance purchase is sometimes required, and you cannot travel during peak times. These fares are usually available only in coach, and the amount you can save differs from one route to another.

- *Tour packages.* These come in an array of combinations; check to see what is available in the area you want to visit. In addition to your train tickets, such packages can include car rental, hotel, bus tours, even cruises. Ask for the booklet describing tours in the section of the country where you will be going.

Domestic train travel with children can be practical and fun for a short trip, with a meal or two in a dining car or perhaps a cabin overnight. But we would not recommend spending more than one day at a time on a train with younger kids. You won't be able to stop at will as you would in a car, and even though the children can walk around, the space will seem more confining as the time drags on. If your children are younger than seven or eight, think hard about using the train for a long haul.

Be advised that "rail fare" covers only the transportation from place to place; for overnight travel, "accommodations charges" are added to the basic fare.

Foreign train travel. Moving from one place to another by train can be efficient, economical, and comfortable in many parts of the world. While airfare price wars and superhighways have become a way of life for Americans, the train has held its position elsewhere as a primary means of transportation. Many countries' rail systems are modern and well maintained, with clean trains and punctual service. In Europe, where distances between cities and even between countries are generally shorter, train travel is quite practical. In many European cities the train station is a hub of activity in the central downtown area; it may offer hotel reservation services, restaurants, bicycle rentals, and much more. In some places, such as in the Andes, there are towns on the rail routes that are inaccessible by roads. Even where the trains are crowded and worn, rail travel may be less stressful than driving on rough roads with unfamiliar rules and signs and, perhaps, reckless native drivers. If you plan to tour abroad, it makes sense to find out if the rail system is the best way to do so.

The national tourist office of the country in question can supply rail information, or it can give you the address of the national railroad so you can write for information directly. What are some of the things to ask?

Are there different class sections on the trains, and what

physical arrangements and amenities does each offer? Despite the comfort of train travel in many countries, more rudimentary conditions are typical in less developed nations. A half-hour ride from Lisbon to the Costa do Sol spent sitting on wooden benches may be fine. But a journey in Sri Lanka throughout which you must stand, strangers' bodies pressed against you, may be less tolerable. In some such cases you may want to ride first class, along with other foreign tourists. As with domestic trains, of course, ask about baggage checking, food, and sleeping accommodations if these things are relevant to you.

Ask for a timetable, fare schedule, and rail system map if one is available. Study these to see how accessible any out-of-the-way places you'd like to visit are, and how long it takes to move from place to place.

Ask if there are different types of fares (children's fares, family plans, excursions). Some countries offer special fare plans that enable you to use the national railroad network as much as you wish for a flat price. With a Eurailpass, good throughout most of Western Europe, you travel by first class as often as you wish, on whatever train routes you wish, for two weeks, a month, or another specified period; children's passes, in addition, are discounted. Similar deals can be found elsewhere, as with the Britrail Pass, good for travel throughout Great Britain, and the Japan Rail Pass. Usually these passes must be purchased before leaving the United States, since they are available only to foreign tourists.

Compare the costs of train travel with your other options. If your itinerary includes covering much ground, a car rental may be cheaper for a family of four than a rail pass. If you plan to base yourselves in one or two European cities for a week or more, however, you will probably save money by taking your side trips by train, buying tickets as needed, rather than by car. Or it may even pay to fly; you may be able to buy intercity flight tickets at reduced prices once you are overseas.

Going places by train abroad offers a wonderful opportunity to meet the native people, especially if you travel in second-class sections. Your children will provide their own introductions, and the experience of sharing impromptu meals and conversation with your fellow travelers may lead to friendships and understanding that last long afterwards. One family we know ended up staying overnight with a Swiss family they met in such circumstances; this hospitality resulted in a continuing friendship over the years.

Abroad as well as in the United States, extensive train travel is generally easier if your kids are older; touring from city to city with luggage may simply be too much for a family with very young children. You might take a train trip once or twice for fun, but to make economical use of a rail pass would probably be emotionally draining.

Going by Car

Whether you should drive rather than use some form of mass transportation will depend on your needs regarding economy, speed, and flexibility. If you take your own car, your biggest concern will be to make the driving experience more manageable and enjoyable; we take up this matter in Chapter 6. If you must rent a car, however, you will first want to know how to get the best deal.

Shop around. Check whether you're eligible for a discount (through an organization you belong to, an employer you work for, or a credit card you have) with one of the big rental companies. In your local phone book you'll probably find toll-free numbers for these companies. You might also check whether your library has a phone book for the city where you'll rent the car. If so, you can call smaller, local companies as well as the big ones. Tourist offices and guidebooks may also provide information on local car rental companies. These businesses may charge less, even than the big companies' discounted prices, although the local companies' cars may be a bit older. Your automobile club, a travel agent, or the tourist office may be able to arrange a well-priced car rental for you. If you are flying, you might check whether the airline offers a fly-drive package; Amtrak offers similar plans for train travelers.

The right car. Decide what size and type of car you want. When we travel with our kids, we prefer a station wagon; if we were renting, we'd probably choose a van or minivan, which is easier to find. In a station wagon or van you can spread out your paraphernalia in the back, with blankets, pillows, toys, and games on top, so that the kids can reach what they need from the back seat without being crowded. But you might prefer a sedan; although the baggage will be harder to get to, it will be safer from theft when you're away from the car.

Next think about what extras you want—automatic transmis-

> *Choosing the size and type of car may be a bit trickier if you are renting abroad; the models are often different from those of the same make at home, and the sizes are generally smaller. "Intermediate" or "compact" cars in other countries may not be the same size as cars given the same designations in the United States. When we arrange a foreign car rental from home, we get the actual interior dimensions of the different rental models available, then we call or visit a local auto dealer and compare the measurements with those of American models.*

sion, radio, tape deck, luggage rack, air conditioning, and the like. These days such features are common in this country, but less so elsewhere. Checking in advance will eliminate surprises. Automatic transmission will mean poorer gas mileage, but may mean more relaxed driving if you prefer not to shift manually. A radio or tape deck can help the time pass for both you and the kids; a radio can introduce you to the local music and give you practice in a foreign language, and a tape deck allows you to play favorite music as well as story tapes for the children. Air conditioning—often unavailable with foreign rentals—can be a godsend for driving in hot areas. It's also easier to hear the radio or tape without the wind blowing in your ears and the sound of passing traffic. Don't forget to reserve a child safety seat for your baby or young child.

Pick-up and drop-off. Find out how much trouble it will be to get and return your car. Will the car be waiting for you at the airport, or will you all have to pile with your luggage into a cab or bus and shlep yourselves to a downtown office?

Cost. To compare various companies' charges, you'll need to ask about the following:

- Is there a mileage charge? One company's higher rental fee that includes unlimited mileage may be less than another's lower base rate plus mileage charge.
- Are there extra charges for extra features? Sometimes there are; sometimes these features are included in the price.
- Are pick-up or drop-off fees added on?
- Are you paying a higher rate to pick up or leave the car at the airport or another convenient location? You might be able to

get the same car for a bit less at an agency located a little farther away.
- Are taxes and insurance costs included? Warning: When you rent a car in Western Europe, the infamous "value-added tax" can be a killer. It adds a quick 15 percent to charges that may already be in the hundreds of dollars.

These general rules apply to automobile rental expenses. Costs per day are usually lower—

- if you rent when business is slower, such as midweek rather than on a weekend, and in low rather than high season;
- if you rent for a longer block of time, such as a week versus a day or two; and
- if the car is smaller and has fewer extras.

When you're comparing costs, be sure that you are comparing the same or similar car models, sizes, and features.

If you're renting a car abroad, keep a few other things in mind. The company may not permit your crossing certain international borders in its car, so you should mention your itinerary when you inquire. Also, there may be additional charges if you pick up the car in one country and drop it off in another, and one country's rental rates may be cheaper than another's.

Important tips. Here are some suggestions for helping to make the rental as hassle-free as you can:

- Make your reservations well ahead of time. You may need to send an advance deposit; in any case, get your reservation confirmed in writing.
- If you want to pay the balance with a personal check when you pick up the car, find out in advance whether the company will accept this.
- If a credit card is required, ask whether you need a certain one, or a minimum credit limit.
- When you pick up the car, look it over carefully. Make sure that you know where everything is and how to operate the horn, lights, and so forth. To avoid questions when you return the car, check also for dents and scratches, and make sure the agent notes them on the rental form. Make sure, too, that all is in working order (the tires are filled, the radio works, seat belts buckle) before you drive off.

- Make sure you have a service number to call if car repairs are needed once you're on the road.

Whenever you travel by car, use seat belts and, for children under four, car seats. In the United States, it's illegal to transport a child without appropriate restraints.

Going by Recreational Vehicle

No members of the travel industry have responded more directly to the needs of traveling families than those who sell and rent recreational vehicles. This is the one form of transportation that has children as well as adults in mind in design and marketing. Whether to make a recreational vehicle part of your vacation depends on where you are going and the style in which you wish to travel. Let's consider some of the pros and cons.

What are the advantages of a recreational vehicle? In one of these things you roam around like the trusty old turtle, always bringing your home along. Transportation and accommodations are in one package, providing a freedom not available with any other form of travel. Lunchtime in the Rockies and no restaurants around? That's okay. You've got your pantry and your kitchen with you. Has the temperature suddenly turned chilly? No need to dig out a suitcase or run back to the motel; just reach into the closet and grab a sweater. Your schedule and pace are as flexible as you care to make them; you can choose to have dinner where you have the best view rather than at whatever restaurant you can find.

Recreational vehicles are particularly suited to outdoors-loving people who would rather spend time in a campground than in a hotel room. The woods or fields become your living room, and at the same time a place to meet other people. Your kids will often find playmates readily available.

Traveling in a recreational vehicle has special advantages when the kids are along. The vehicle is literally their home away from home; it becomes familiar and secure, and they need not adjust repeatedly to new beds in new places. You don't have to pack and unpack—a luxury on a long tour. All the little things they frequently want on the road are at hand: the favorite toy, a drink of water, even a toilet when there isn't a gas station in sight. You need not worry about finding things for them to eat on restaurant menus; you can cook what they like.

If you already own an RV, using it can be an economical way to travel. The extra you spend on gasoline will be more than made up for by your savings on lodgings and food.

What are the disadvantages of a recreational vehicle? RV rental costs can be pretty steep. Add in the cost of gas—the larger ones are real gas hogs—and the expense for tooling around in an RV may be just too great. Be sure to weigh those costs against what you will save; for instance, if you will be visiting friends or relatives who wouldn't mind putting you up, an ordinary car might make more sense for you.

An RV can be a bit of a burden at times. It may be difficult to park in a large city, where it will be very inviting to thieves. When possible, leave your RV in an attended parking lot. You can ask a policeman or the tourist office where to find such lots convenient to the places you'll be visiting; you can even obtain this information ahead of time, by asking the tourist office to mark attended lots on the city map they'll be sending. In some countries, you may often find campgrounds within or on the edges of major cities. In such cases, you can leave the RV in the campground and get around by public transportation.

Living within the confines of an RV may not be to everyone's taste. Driving all day and spending the evening in the same space may feel too restricting to you, or provide a bit more togetherness than you and your kids prefer. If you like the out-of-doors best on TV, and the crisp night air and the hooting of an owl make you feel crawly, RV travel may not be the way to go. Nor is it the best choice for someone who wants to be waited on. Life in an RV generally requires some cooking, dishwashing, and housekeeping, or that gleaming and efficient space can turn all too quickly into a cramped hovel.

What can you get in a recreational vehicle? As much as you are willing to pay for. A small camper will provide sleeping space for three or four, a foldaway table, storage space, sink, stove, and icebox. A mini–motor home will accommodate four or five people, with a refrigerator rather than an icebox, and toilet and shower as well. You can continue up the ladder; some motor homes sleep eight and offer a full kitchen, air conditioning, tub and shower, and sofa.

Recreational vehicles abroad tend to be a bit smaller than those in the United States, although you can easily find very comfortable ones. The interiors may also be set up differently in foreign models. Whether you rent here or overseas, start by writing various agencies for brochures. These will have diagrams of interior layouts, with dimensions. If possible, visit a local dealer to see for yourself how these diagrams translate into real life. This can also help you envision a foreign model with a different layout. One European firm, for example, offers a mini–motor home in a Volkswagen van; it sleeps five and includes a toilet, shower, and refrigerator. This may sound terrific, but if you look inside a VW camper van you will quickly get an idea of how tight the space may be.

While checking on available units and prices, ask about a few other things as well.

- Is there inside access from the driving cab to the living area? A unit that requires you to go outside and around is more problematic. Those in the cab are cut off from those in the camper while driving.
- Will the rental company supply utensils, dishes, pots and pans, pillows, sleeping bags or blankets, bed linens, and towels? These items may be included in the rental or offered at an additional charge, or you may have to supply them yourself.
- Ask whether stoves and refrigerators are powered by propane gas or electricity, and find out if propane and campground electrical outlets are available in the area you will be touring. Ask about water storage and sewage tanks. In general, find out how all the equipment works.
- Get gas mileage figures and average gasoline prices for the country or region you plan to tour. (In many countries gas prices are double or triple those in the United States.)
- Ask what insurance is included in the rental cost, the amount of the deductible portion, and the availability and cost of extra coverage.

Where can you rent a recreational vehicle? Tourist offices here and abroad may be able to provide you with the names of local companies. You can write to the companies directly for brochures and information. Abroad, the same companies that rent cars often rent motor homes and smaller RVs as well. The addresses of some of these foreign car rental agencies are listed in the Appendix, as are the names and addresses of some foreign and domestic companies that rent only RVs. If you'll be starting your RV tour from home, look in your yellow pages under "recreational vehicles" and "motor homes" for agencies near you. You can also ask your automobile club for the names of rental agencies, or book your RV through a travel agent.

A final caution: When you pick up your vehicle, have someone show you how everything works, and make sure that everything you need is aboard. A failure to notice that we were missing the electrical cable in a European rental left us without electricity until we located one—a week and two countries later.

CHAPTER FIVE

Packing for the Trip

WE COULDN'T POSSIBLY give you a complete list of things you should pack to take with you on your family trip; that would be like trying to tell you what diet you should follow without knowing anything about you. You'll need to consider the type of trip you have planned (city touring or wilderness camping? beach cottage or luxury resort?), the climate where you will be, how much you want to carry, the type of transportation you'll be using, and whether you are willing to do some laundry.

Packing well takes some practice. If you want to travel as light as possible while still covering all the eventualities, approach the task in an organized way. As far ahead as you can, make a packing list for each member of the family, keeping in mind the requirements of the trip. Include toiletries and medicines as well as clothing. Keep adding to the lists as you remember essential items. This will alert you to things you may need to buy for the trip. When the time comes to pack, your lists will translate into separate piles for each person.

Clothing

For any trip of longer than a week, we pack as if we were going for one week, and plan on a weekly wash. Some packing guides advise taking fewer pairs of socks or underwear and washing them out in the sink. That's fine if you wish to. But such items really don't take up much suitcase room; they fit nicely into crannies and inside shoes. So we take a week's worth of them as well.

These guidelines may help you in deciding what clothes to bring along:

- Take clothes that can serve multiple purposes. Pack beach thongs the kids can also use as bedroom slippers, a raincoat that looks good enough for evening wear, a skirt that goes with a casual sweater or dressy blouse. Don't take two things if one will do the job of both.
- Take clothes in a couple of basic colors for each person. If the colors and patterns of the garments are simple and compatible, they can be combined to make a variety of outfits.
- Take clothes with strong colors and printed patterns, to hide dirt and stains.
- Take clothes that can be layered. A sundress with a blouse underneath becomes a jumper. A sweater or jacket over a light shirt can be peeled off if the airplane cabin is too warm and put back on when you arrive during the cool evening. Try to anticipate temperature differences between your home and your destination, and from place to place during each day.
- Take wash-and-wear, wrinkle-resistant clothes. These will look the best with the least amount of care.
- Choose clothes that dry quickly, in case no automatic dryer is available.
- Take familiar, comfortable clothes. If you must buy some new things for the trip, do so well in advance and try them out first at home. You want clothes that will allow you and the children to curl up comfortably for a nap, and that won't bind in case of an upset tummy. Comfort is especially important when it comes to shoes; both adults and children should have broken-in and comfortable old friends on their feet.

Baby Things

Packing for an infant can be daunting. The baby will need more changes of clothing than anyone else, although, since baby clothes are small, they generally pack compactly. Other baby things can take a lot of space, depending on your parenting style and where you're going.

If you use baby food, formula, or disposable diapers, take a few days' supply; later you can shop for more. If you are headed overseas where the right food or formula may not be available, you may need to take more. (Tourist offices can usually tell you whether what you need can be bought where you're going.) Canned, ready-to-use formula saves the trouble of preparation, and is especially useful in places where water quality is questionable. (If you're flying, call the airline to find out the best way to take along cases of formula.) In general, if there are cities on your itinerary, it makes sense to take a limited amount of consumable supplies and restock as you go.

Most hotels and motels make crib sheets and blankets available. A beach cottage may not, even if a crib is provided, so you may want to take your own.

Have a waterproof changing sheet so you can change the little one without soaking the hotel bed or your lap. A plastic sheet that can be sponged off is most convenient; a flannel-coated rubber sheet will serve the purpose but will need to be washed, and it can't go in a hot dryer.

A collapsible stroller can be a lifesaver. Look for the type that weighs just a few pounds and can be carried over your arm, taken easily on and off planes, trains, and busses, and fit into small spaces.

You may prefer a baby sling, a backpack for an older infant or toddler, or a frontpack for a younger infant who isn't yet able to sit. Such carriers are especially useful for hiking or strolling off the sidewalks. Frameless cloth carriers fold up into almost nothing, and backpacks with frames usually include storage pouches for diapers, wallet, and so on.

For a baby who can't sit on his own yet, an infant seat provides somewhere to put him down and to feed him. His car seat, however, can double for this purpose.

A small bassinet, car bed, or infant bed can be carried along on any type of conveyance and can provide a place for the baby to sleep in transit, in a hotel or guest house without a crib, in a tent, or in a rented house. If you are driving, you might instead bring a portable crib or small playpen (which can double as bed and play area), but these things are too big to lug on trains and airplanes.

In the woods or at the beach, have some mosquito netting to cover the baby's bed or playpen. And be sure to take a sun hat and a beach umbrella if you plan to spend hot days in the sun.

Some Useful Extras

The following are some items you might not have thought to bring along. They are not things you necessarily must have, but they can come in mighty handy:

- a travel alarm clock (get one that folds safely into its own case);
- a Swiss Army knife, with can and bottle opener, screwdriver, and so on;
- a clothes brush or roll of sticky tape, for lint removal;
- a small sewing kit for little emergencies;
- nail clippers or nail scissors;
- two or more large plastic bags for dirty laundry;
- a small flashlight for the bedside table, to light the way in unfamiliar territory;
- soap, in case it's not provided;
- a compact first-aid kit (see Chapter 10);
- small cellophane-wrapped packets of tissues; and
- disposable damp cloths.

Actually, we consider the last three items *necessities* when we travel with kids.

Don't forget to pack toys, snacks, and drinks; a good assortment will make for a smooth trip. See Chapter 6 for details.

If you're going abroad, you may need adapters and converters for electrical appliances. An adapter fits onto your appliance plug so that you can use different-shaped sockets. A converter attaches to your appliance to correct for the difference between American electric voltage (110 volts) and that elsewhere (which may be 220 volts). The type of converter you need depends on your appliance and how many watts of electricity it uses; check the written information that comes with your appliance. (Some appliances can handle either voltage; you change from one to the other with a flick of the switch. But even for these you need a plug adapter.)

Before you plug into a foreign outlet, or one on a cruiseship, check to see if it's 110 or 220 volts. You don't need your converter if it's 110; if you use the converter, in fact, you may ruin both it and the appliance. Also, converters don't work on DC current, so ask the tourist office or travel agent about the electrical systems of the country you will visit. And since American appliances operating on foreign currents may run slower, bring a wind-up or battery-powered clock instead of one that must be plugged in.

What Not to Take

- *Duplicate items.* Share toothpaste, soap, shampoo, and lotions, and whatever else you can think of. The kids should pick toys and games that appeal to more than one of them.
- *Unnecessary dressy clothing.* Little boys rarely need ties; Dad can usually manage with just one. Clothes that can be dressed up when necessary are more useful than those you can wear only on dressy occasions.
- *Expensive jewelry.* Unless you need it for a specific purpose, leave it at home where you won't have to worry about it.
- *Unnecessary variety.* You may be bored wearing the same clothes over and over again, but if you are going from place to place nobody else will notice, and you'll be traveling much lighter. The kids will need more changes of clothing, of course, to last until washday.

The Luggage

How big should it be? When we first traveled with our children, we packed as much as possible into a couple of very large suitcases, assuming that the fewer objects to manipulate the better. After dragging those monsters around vast airports and contemplating arm transplants, we changed our minds. Since then we have found three or four smaller cases to be more suitable than one or two huge ones. Besides weighing less and letting you balance your load, they make it easier to organize and find your things. We pack each person's clothing separately, so we can get to whatever we need quickly without rummaging through everyone's things.

Hard versus soft. There are benefits to both: Hard luggage is generally more resistant to the wear and tear of baggage handling on trains and planes, and may last longer because of its durable construction. Soft luggage, though, is lighter, can fit more easily into the nooks and crannies of your vehicle, and gives to accommodate an extra sweater or some souvenirs.

> *On most flights each passenger is allowed to take two bags not greater than 62 inches (the total of height, length, and width added together; the second will need to be smaller on some airlines). Sixty-two inches is the size of an average Pullman suitcase. The weight of each bag should not exceed 70 pounds. You will be charged extra for oversized or overweight bags.*
>
> *To fit under the seat on most airplanes, carry-on bags should be no more than 45 inches (again, the total of height, length, and width).*
>
> *Other forms of public transportation may also have baggage limits, so check when making your reservations.*

Smaller bags. Whether you're strolling the Champs Élysées, hiking in the Rockies, or lallygagging on the beach in Florida, you'll need a carrying bag, or more than one, to hold snacks, maps, and other things that go with you everywhere. When you travel by plane or train, such a bag will be your carry-on luggage. A shoulder bag, roomy but not burdensomely big, may prove indispensable. Some parents use a diaper bag with multiple compartments for this general purpose.

Most practical for a touring vacation may be a large pocketbook or shoulder bag. It should have a number of separate compartments, and they should close securely with zippers, not snaps. One pocket can be reserved for important papers like passports, travel vouchers, and travelers' checks. This compartment should be the one that seems safest, perhaps the one that is always against the body. Another pocket may hold your wallet and personal things. A third can be reserved for things the kids may need—tissues, lip balm, disposable wipes, Life Savers, gum, maybe a few small toys or a small notepad and pencil to be pulled out in places like restaurants. Reserve a space for any frequently used medicines. Many bags have nonfastening front pockets that are just right for holding street maps, guidebooks, currency converters, and so forth.

A large canvas or nylon tote bag is also very useful, for taking towels and sunscreen to the beach or for carrying little necessities from car to room and back again. Many have pockets for small things. These bags tend to be a bit bulky to use while touring.

Whenever you travel, have all your luggage clearly tagged with your name, address, and phone number. Use sturdy tags, like the ones enclosed in plastic or vinyl cases, and attach them securely to your bags. To discourage burglary while you're away, use a business address rather than your home address.

For a hike through the woods, or a full day at Disneyland when you will want your sweaters as evening comes on, a day pack comes in handy. You can transfer what you need into such a pack and leave your hands free. When you don't need it, the pack can be easily folded and put away in a suitcase.

Also easily stowed away when not needed are smaller cloth bags with handles. They can serve as carry-on luggage, making snacks, sweater, and books and magazines easily accessible; as shopping bags; or simply as extra bags when all the others are full.

For most trips, we recommend taking one medium-sized suitcase for each adult or teenager or two smaller kids, one large pocketbook and a larger carrying bag to be carried by the adults, and a cloth bag or day pack for each child. Add a suit bag if you'll need dressy clothes.

Remove any old airline tags before checking your baggage (or make sure the agent removes them), and look at the tags the agent puts on to make sure your luggage will go on the same vacation you do. It's also a good idea to mark your suitcases with stickers or colored tape to differentiate them from other bags of the same appearance. This could keep some fellow passenger from mistakenly grabbing your luggage off the conveyer belt and rushing off with it to make his connecting flight to Tibet.

CHAPTER SIX
Managing en Route

GETTING TO WHERE you are going should be a fun part of your vacation, not a headache. There are things you can do to make plane, train, or car travel with kids a pleasure.

Set the Mood

To ensure a carefree drive or flight, get everyone in a relaxed frame of mind before you go. You'll all be excited and a little tense as you get ready to leave, of course, but channeling these feelings into constructive activity and pleasant anticipation will help you avoid conflict and needless stress.

Get ready early. The first step in preventing disaster on the day of departure is to do as much ahead as possible. Finish packing the day before you are to leave. Have your bags sitting by the front door to avoid charging about when it's time to go; even carry-on luggage and the things you will be using in the car can be put with the luggage. Have at hand a list of items that cannot be packed until the last moment (toothbrushes, little Angie's favorite stuffed animal), and put the list in a prominent place with the bags. If you are going by car and have a garage that locks, pack the car the night before. Do all the necessary automobile checks (oil, tire pressure, gas fill-up) ahead as well. Doing all these things in advance will leave you time to get a good night's sleep, and to reconsider if you find you are taking too much to carry, or if the load distribution might be improved. These adjustments are a routine part of any trip; they're only a hassle if you are in a rush.

Share the preparations. If you can get everybody to help, the kids will feel involved, and you'll be building the sense of cooperation and fellowship that you want to carry through the trip. Find things, however simple, for each family member to do. Even a very young child can be given a little task, like assembling favorite objects to go in the carry-on luggage (as long as this is being done early, you will have time for diplomatic talks about that four-foot mountain of stuffed animals).

Create a relaxed atmosphere. Do everything you can to encourage a feeling of ease for a full day before departure. Don't overwork the kids with last-minute preparations; give them time to play, and take a break to sit quietly with them and talk about the upcoming events. See that everyone gets plenty of sleep on the night before the trip. Try also to make meals happy on the day of departure; avoid foods that might cause battles of will or upset tummies.

Things to Have Handy en Route

Clothes. For younger kids and, especially, infants, it's wise to have a change of clothes readily at hand in case of spills. Have the clothes in your carry-on bag when taking a plane or train. For car travel, the extra duds can be kept in an accessible suitcase—but keep them together at the top where you can get at them quickly.

Baby things. Pack the diaper bag with whatever you'll need for the day, or until you can reload. Don't forget damp cloths for cleanup, plastic bags to hold wet or soiled clothes and diapers, a full change of clothes, and a changing sheet or pad. Even if you'll be using cloth diapers on your trip, you'll probably want to include a few disposables to avoid frequent diaper changes, particularly where they're awkward, as on an airplane.

Gum and candy. When you're flying, air pressure changes can block up the ears and cause discomfort to kids. Sucking, chewing, and swallowing can help, so take along chewing gum or hard candies for takeoffs, landings, or whenever your child's ears are bothered by pressure during the flight. Similar pressure in the ears may be felt when driving mountain roads that subject you to altitude changes. Here the changes may be slower, but again candy or gum can come in handy.

Drinks. Thirst is another minor irritation that may occur in transit. (Statistics show that if you travel with three children in a car and stop for a drink each time one of them is thirsty, you can cover as much as four miles in a single day's driving.) Here again a piece of hard candy can help for a little while, if you have nothing to drink. On a car trip, bring a Thermos or canteen (perhaps more than one) full of liquid, or individual water, juice, or soda containers that you can throw away as they are used. Juices in small boxes, complete with straws, store handily and need no refrigeration, and the empty boxes can be crumpled up for easy disposal. On a long, hot drive, you may want to bring a large insulated container of water, with a lot of ice added before departure.

Snacks. However you travel, a few snacks may come in handy at difficult times. Maybe your child gets hungriest between meals regardless of when you stop to eat, cannot wait another minute to eat even though the plane hasn't even taken off yet, or absolutely detests the lunch served on board. Hunger aside, having a snack gives the little ones something to do to help the time pass en route.

Try to choose snacks that aren't too messy. Sticky or juicy foods that will be with you for the duration of the trip in the form of spots and hand prints on the upholstery won't do a lot for your disposition. Also try to avoid too many sweet things, which may lead to uneaten dinners. You might fill small plastic bags with dry cereal, nuts, raisins, or dried fruits, or buy ready-made "trail mix." Crackers can be carried along easily, and augmented with cheese and fresh fruits.

Be sure to have appropriate snacks on hand for your older baby as well. Crackers and teething biscuits will satisfy his need to chew.

Medicines. If anyone in the family routinely takes some medication, it should be carried along in Mother's pocketbook or some other very convenient place. In addition, if your child tends to easily develop earaches, headaches, colds, or the like, carry along those medicines you would ordinarily administer. Do the same for adults in the family who are prone to certain discomforts. We shall say a lot about health concerns when traveling in Chapter 10.

Toys. Having a good assortment of toys, games, and materials for activities will go far toward helping a long journey pass swiftly and happily. The things you take should fit several important criteria.

Size. If toys are compact you'll have room for more, and the more variety you have the less likely your children are to be bored. Smaller things can also be used in cramped spaces like car or train seats without disturbing others.

Packing compact, light toys will make it easier for your children to take responsibility for carrying and caring for their own things. Besides freeing you up a bit, their toting their own paraphernalia will help build their sense of responsibility. Even a young child can carry a small day pack on his back (use the kind where the straps meet in the back, so it doesn't slip off), or tote a cloth bag with handles. The size of the pack can form a natural limit on the amount of toys the child can take.

Versatility. Look for toys or objects that can do more than one thing. With a deck of cards you can play war, go fish, old maid, hearts, and many other games. A number of small computer game sets are on the market; they're pricey, so get one that offers several games. Look for small, magnetized games designed for travel; again, one set may combine several games, such as chess, checkers, and backgammon.

A pad of paper and some crayons or pencils remain one of the most versatile diversions for any child. She can draw to her heart's content and then play tic-tac-toe or hangman. You can make up your own activities as well. Draw a numeral and have your child make a picture from it; make your own rebuses; invent a dot-to-dot picture for your child to complete. A magnetized drawing board such as Etch-a-Sketch, or the kind of pad where the picture disappears when you lift the cellophane, is also good fun.

Small plastic figures (soldiers, space creatures, animals, and the like) can be used to make up all sorts of games and stories. They also fit easily into little corners of a child's pack. Small building toys are also versatile in that they can be used over and over to make any number of different things, without requiring much space. Bring enough to make a small building but not enough to scatter in the airplane aisle for people to step on. Choose blocks or straws that interlock in some way, and pick the larger-sized versions (Duplos instead of Legos, for example).

Variety. Select toys and materials that together will suit different needs at different times. Include—

- games that can be played between parent and child or between children;
- solo activities and games—puzzles, activity books, coloring books, and so forth;
- building toys, especially for a young child;
- books, both for parents to read aloud and for a child to read alone;
- craft materials that aren't messy (you might teach your child knitting, crocheting, or macrame in the weeks before the trip, and provide a small new ball of yarn);
- toys for active play during breaks in travel—a sturdy balloon or inflatable ball, a small Frisbee, or a jump rope (stow such things away when they're not appropriate);
- a small radio or tape player and tapes, and earphones; and
- for the baby, little toys with nondetachable moving parts; a doll, stuffed toy, or hand puppet; a toy that makes noise (not too much). An older baby may also like looking at cardboard or cloth books with Mommy or Daddy.

The Plane Ride

There is a feeling of frenzy in any large, busy airport that anyone who has rushed from cab to ticket counter to gate with one worried eye on the clock understands. You can do without that feeling when you have the whole family along. Things may go more smoothly if you and your spouse split up the chores: One of you can check the baggage while the other supervises bathroom visits and drinks of water, or you can each take responsibility for a particular child. Whichever way you decide to share the load, the important thing is to do it purposefully, setting a cooperative tone for the whole trip.

Get to the airport fifteen or twenty minutes earlier than you would if you were traveling alone. If you arrive earlier than this, you run the risk of having too much time to hang around in the terminal. Always call the airline before leaving home to see if there are any known delays, so you can do your waiting at home instead.

If there is a wait at the check-in counter or a sizable walk from that point to the departure gate, one of you should head off with the kids for the gate. Kids would rather do almost anything than stand and wait, and this enables them to amble along at a leisurely pace. Once at the gate you can all relax in comfortable chairs.

Some foreign airports provide nursery areas for passengers traveling with infants. Here you may find cribs, playpens, and possibly even washing machines. Such facilities are rarely available in the United States, though many have diapering rooms near the restrooms.

Airlines usually board families first to give them extra time to get the kids settled in. A relaxed preparation for takeoff helps to promote the calm mood you want. If your kids are older, though, they may not need the extra time and might prefer not having to sit on the plane longer than necessary.

Whatever seating arrangement you have chosen, make sure that each parent can share actively in child management in flight. If the size of your family or a shortage of seats necessitates splitting up, consider switching seats with your spouse during the flight; this can be a refreshing change for both parents and kids. Have each child's bag of toys and materials handy, and gum, candy, or bottle ready if needed to unclog ears.

If your baby is going to need formula or food warmed up, tell the flight attendant as soon as you are in the air. This courtesy will help the staff plan around their other tasks.

The airlines offer a variety of amenities that can help children pass the time in the air pleasantly. Many airlines give packets of little toys, games, and puzzles to children on board; whatever the packets contain, kids welcome them for their novelty. The kids may also be given a pair of plastic pilot's wings to wear proudly on their chests, and you can sometimes obtain playing cards on board, in case you didn't bring any. Stereo provides a welcome distraction when it is available. Whether they're listening to a special children's channel or to some other kind of music, the kids will relax and be entertained. They can draw, color, or even sleep while they listen.

Movies can be entertaining for older children. For the really little ones they serve a different purpose: With the passengers quiet, the lights turned off, and the shades pulled down, your child may fall asleep to the quiet hum of the engines. Be prepared for this; ask for a blanket and pillow at the beginning of the flight. If there are empty seats, your little one may be able to stretch out across them if you lift up the armrest in between; or you can offer your lap as a pillow. Earphones cost several dollars on movie flights, but they can be worth the expense.

Try to be tolerant if your little one refuses to eat the food served on board, even if you ordered a special meal of hot dog and milkshake. If he's hungry twenty minutes later, you can feel smug as you whip out your snack bag. A selection of fruit juices, soft drinks, and milk is usually available in the galley even between meals.

In case you discover at 40,000 feet that your infant meal didn't make it on board, have spare jars of baby food along in your carry-on bags.

Help your children to space their activities so that they don't become bored or restless. Intersperse games or art projects with snacks or meals; read a story, then take a brief stroll up and down the aisle. There are stretching exercises you can do together even while seated; some airlines offer pamphlets describing them. Take a bathroom break, then encourage the kids to watch the movie for a while or close their eyes and listen to music (you needn't say what you hope will happen). When they decide to switch activities, suggest something that will call on different skills or interests; a little variety will keep them interested for longer.

If you organized properly you didn't have to rush to board the plane; there's no need to do so getting off, either. When the plane lands, it will be easier to manage if you adopt the attitude that a few minutes won't matter. (They won't; you'll have to wait at the baggage area anyway.)

Have one parent act as the "designated checker," who quickly scans planes, trains, cabs, or airport waiting rooms for any dropped articles as the family leaves. The two of you can take turns at this job. Just be sure you know whose turn it is.

The Train Ride

Here are a few tips for making your train trip more enjoyable:
- Make sure your child has access to a hard, flat surface for writing or drawing. If meals are served on trays, your child may be able to use one of those. Drop-down tables are provided on some long-distance trains. If there is a dinette or club car, you can take your child there to use the tables and enjoy a change of scenery. A fold-out or detachable table may be provided along with sleeping accommodations. But probably the safest thing is to carry along something that can serve as a lap desk.
- A portable tape player can be a useful additon to your child's bag of travel things. Use earphones to avoid disturbing fellow passengers.
- Bring a little pillow and blanket if your child needs a nap and you don't have sleeping accommodations. Abroad, your tot may be able to stretch across a bench seat for a nap; on an American train her seat may recline.
- Bring snacks and drinks in disposable containers, or even bring a picnic lunch; it's relatively easy to manage eating at your seats.
- Take advantage of the meal service to break the monotony of train travel; going to the dining car for dinner is like going out to a restaurant. You are likely to find menu items that appeal to the children, and child-size portions are available. Your child may even be given an activity to keep him occupied as he waits for his dinner.
- Keep your tickets. You will need them for making connections or getting back on the train after a layover. In some countries you must turn in the ticket at the end of your journey.
- Keep your passports in a convenient place when going by train between countries. You may not be aware that you are crossing a border, and you'll want your passports handy when an official steps into your compartment and asks to see them.
- If you are touring by train, try not to schedule back-to-back days of train travel. Break up the trip with some free days in between.
- Enjoy the relative spaciousness of a train. Take the kids for an occasional walk.

On the Road

Things to take along. In a car or RV, you don't have to worry quite so much about ease of carrying and packing toys and the like.

Though it is a convenience to have these things together in one handy receptacle, the receptacle can be a plastic bag on the seat with the child, a box on the car floor, or, in a station wagon or van, a small suitcase left unzipped behind the kids' seats. Some easy means of carrying the kids' stuff from car to motel room does help, but in a car or RV you certainly don't need to concern yourself with neatness as much as you would on a plane or train.

A recreational vehicle provides kids more freedom to spread out than any other type of transportation. Not only is there closet and drawer space, but suitcases or bags of stuff can be put in a corner and not have to be moved much at all, and you won't need to carry the kids' things from vehicle to room at night.

Be sure to have a blanket and pillow reachable for naps during the drive. Any small pillow will do, or you can try a small inflatable pillow that can be folded away when not in use. (You may need more than one to prevent arguments.)

The children will also appreciate some hard surface to write on. This can be a thick pad of paper with cardboard backing, a chalkboard, a large picture book, a clipboard, or a lap tray with folding legs. Many stores sell a tray attached to a bean-bag pillow base, which is quite stable and can double as a pillow.

The flexibility and privacy of a car or recreational vehicle gives you more leeway both in what play materials you take and the activities the kids can do en route. You can bring a larger board game or two, though you should try to avoid things that will tip and slide too much. One useful item is Colorforms, a set of soft plastic shapes that stick to a board, allowing kids to make up endless numbers of scenes or structures.

On long car trips, a "secret tape" magically appears in our tape box, with voices that sound suspiciously like our own singing songs, telling stories, jokes, and riddles, and even asking the kids questions to which they can respond. The kids become totally involved with this ruse, and happily try to trick us into admitting our part in it. Their favorite part comes at the end of every tape when they are instructed to open the glove compartment. Lo and behold! A treat for each of them appears as magically as the tape itself.

If the vehicle you are driving doesn't have a tape deck or CD player, you might bring along an inexpensive tape player, and perhaps even earphones. From a symphony to lull the young ones to children's music they can sing along with or popular music that the whole family enjoys, tapes help the time pass quickly. Story tapes are readily available as well, some of them with picture books to be read along with the tape. If you're tired of the tapes you have at home, borrow some from the public library before your trip (check the adult section for classics by such authors as Poe, Dickens, and Sir Arthur Conan Doyle).

Another good car activity is keeping a trip diary. This can be nice for the kids to do no matter how you travel, but it is particularly suited to car or RV travel because they'll have more time to do it. They'll need only a notebook and some tape (better than paste for working in the car). Postcards, matchbook covers, soap wrappers from hotels, or nature objects from the different places you go can be taped into the book, and the whole family can participate in writing memories and impressions next to them. Older kids can carry an inexpensive camera and take pictures to be added later, writing as they go and leaving space for the snapshot. When the trip has ended, the children will have a memory book they can review with pleasure in years to come.

Make your own "Travel Bingo" game for long car trips. Draw symbols for twenty-five things to look for—five rows of five—on a different "board" for each player, or copies of the same one. When the kids see a blue VW, a woman with a hat, a boy with a dog, a boat, a train, or a cow, they cross out the picture; otherwise they play by bingo rules.

Managing on the road. A long day's drive with four or five people can be trying, even in a larger RV. Here are some strategies for managing in that small space:

- Don't overdo the driving. Five to six hours in the car in one day is plenty for us; know your own family's limit. Remember that what's tolerable for the driver may not be for the kids.
- If you can help it, don't put two long driving days back to back. Spend a day in between at a beach or an amusement park. If there is no such attraction on the route, at least stop early enough on one of the days to do something fun—swim in a motel pool, explore a town, find a park or playground, go to a movie.

Nothing is more deadly to the vacation spirit than a daily regimen of "drive, eat, sleep."

- Stop every couple of hours or so to break up the tedium. And don't spend every break just sitting in a restaurant. Try to do something physical—stretch, play catch, or, if it's raining, go into a tourist information center and bat a toy balloon around for a while.

Put all the swimming things in one small duffel bag or pack, so you don't have to go digging if you decide to stop for a swim. Include a comb, shampoo, and conditioner (one of each for ladies and for gents) for the after-swim shower.

- Don't arrive places at night. If you do, you'll not only run the risk that your room will be given away or all the restaurants closed, but you'll promote end-of-the-day fatigue and grouchiness. Both kids and parents need some time to unwind, eat dinner, and enjoy a few pleasant hours before bed.
- Find the driving schedule that works best for your family. Drive during usual nap times—you can't do much else anyway, and the nap will refresh your child for the remainder of the day. If he doesn't usually nap, driving in the afternoon may put him to sleep anyway. Also, if your family doesn't get hungry for breakfast until they've been up awhile, try driving for an hour or so as soon as you are up, stopping for breakfast later. This can be a painless way to cover some miles while everyone slowly wakes up, and it may result in a cheerful breakfast instead of all of you gazing blearily into space as you eat.
- To break up long driving spells, choose routes that will take you near interesting places to visit—a historical site, a pretzel factory, a lake you can swim in. Check your guidebooks for such attractions.
- Instead of sitting in a restaurant to eat, pick up some food at a store or roadside stand and find a spot where you can picnic. This allows you some fresh air and the kids some space to move. And picnicking is a great way to sample the flavor of a region.
- In an RV, picnics are a cinch, since the ingredients are always aboard. But picnicking all the time can get tiresome, especially for the cook. Go occasionally to a restaurant for change of pace.

- Make sure you and your spouse each have time to relax and watch the scenery. On long trips we've sometimes argued about who gets to drive just because we both want to avoid having to tend the kids. Bringing along toys, games, and books with which the children can entertain themselves really helps. You may have to remind them that they have such things—"Now it's quiet time; choose something you can do by yourself. In twenty minutes Daddy will play a game with you."
- When things go wrong, adapt. Suppose that five days into a car tour of New England you realize that you are not enjoying yourself. What's wrong? The first place to look is at your itinerary; most people, on car trips, try to do too much in the time allotted. Will it help to get the kids a new toy, or to make more frequent and interesting stops? If minor adjustments don't alleviate the frustration, grit you teeth and cut something out of the schedule. Your pace can slow down, and so can your blood pressure. Take advantage of the flexibility inherent in car travel.

You will without a doubt run into those moments when Jessie simply refuses to entertain herself. Don't be discouraged; just tell your spouse very insistently that it's your turn to drive.

CHAPTER SEVEN

Lodgings—Choosing Them, Enjoying Them

THE RED BALL OF SUN dips below the horizon, sending sparkles of gold dancing across the azure water. You sit on your crumbling veranda, the sounds of dripping plumbing behind you, your nose assaulted by a musty odor that lends your room the aura of a mausoleum. Your repose is occasionally shattered by a car whooshing past on the highway below that separates your hotel from the beach. Faintly, through it all, come the sounds of calypso, and you imagine that you can even hear the clinking cocktail glasses and laughter of the guests at that beach-front luxury hotel just a hundred yards and ten dollars a night away.

Where you stay can make or break a vacation. Whether you're spending a week at a resort hotel, making a few days' stopover at a downtown hotel, or catching a night's sleep just off the highway, finding a place with the ambiance you want and the facilities you prefer will take careful choosing—and having your kids along makes your decision even more crucial. Knowing what's available is the first step toward an intelligent choice.

Guidebooks of different sorts can help you. A good regional guidebook describes the various types of accommodations that are available and the flavor of the different areas where they may be found, and may give detailed descriptions of lodging places with special qualities. Some books can help you find special accommodations, in American country inns, for example, or in castles, manor houses, farms, and other out-of-the-ordinary places abroad.

A tourist office can usually give you an extensive list of places to stay in a particular region, with costs and amenities noted, but such a list won't provide the critical commentaries found in guidebooks. Still, the list may be very useful if you use it along with a regional guidebook.

A city map can help you to determine the location of a given hostelry. Some guidebooks include maps, and tourist offices often provide them. That perfect hotel won't seem so perfect if you discover that it's a twenty-dollar cab ride away from everything you want to see.

A travel agent may help you find suitable lodgings, although it's usually wise to check the guidebooks first. Some agents know only about big hotels, and aren't aware of alternatives. If an agent recommends a place you can't remember reading about, don't hesitate to go home and check it out in your books before you sign on the dotted line.

In thinking about various forms of homes away from home, remember that the options vary considerably depending upon what part of the world you are talking about. Keeping that in mind, let's look at some of the general types available.

Hotels and Motels

Hotels and motels offer service as well as shelter—someone else to make the bed, clean the bathroom, and wash the towels. Beyond these basics, the range of amenities provided varies widely; you can generally find whatever level of comfort or splendor you prefer.

Hotels and motels are also familiar and convenient. No matter what continent or country you are traversing, the experience of staying in a hotel will remain pretty much the same—no culture shock here. And it's fairly easy to find a suitable hotel or motel in the middle of the city or at the highway exit ramp.

And although hotels and motels provide a lot of service, this service is usually quite impersonal. If you seek restful anonymity, this can be attractive.

These general types of hotels and motels may be available:

The chains. Their familiar signs dot the landscape; stay in one once and you've stayed in them all. Within this category, though, are several grades of expense and comfort.

Budget motels range from spartan to quite well equipped. The budget motel may not have its own restaurant or coffee shop, but it may have an outdoor swimming pool. Budget motels may charge by the number of persons in a room; a base price for a single person is increased by a small amount for each additional occupant. Children often pay a reduced rate, and those under two may be free. Thanks to fierce competition, some budget motels even allow all kids under seventeen or eighteen to stay free, and some provide continental breakfast at no charge.

Moderate to expensive chains offer more amenities. Most have a restaurant of some type—at least a coffee shop, usually a family restaurant, but possibly a posh dining room or even a nightclub. Swimming pools, exercise rooms, and saunas have all become commonplace in moderate and higher-priced chains. Many chain hotels and motels offer babysitting services. Other amenities—tennis courts, a concierge to get your theater tickets, a maid to turn down your bed at night—are available at more expensive hotels and motels.

Most chains are quite predictable from link to link, but there are exceptions. Whereas a hotel near the airport may be modest in price and appearance, one by the same name downtown may have an opulent lobby and a haute cuisine restaurant.

Most rooms in moderate to expensive chains have two double beds. Usually, children under a specified age are allowed to stay for free in the same room with their parents. There may be a small extra charge if a cot or a crib is brought in.

Information about most chains, from budget to imperial, is readily available. Call the toll-free reservation number and ask for a directory; it will list locations, prices, and amenities for each link in the chain. Or ask the reservations clerk to tell you what the place does and does not have.

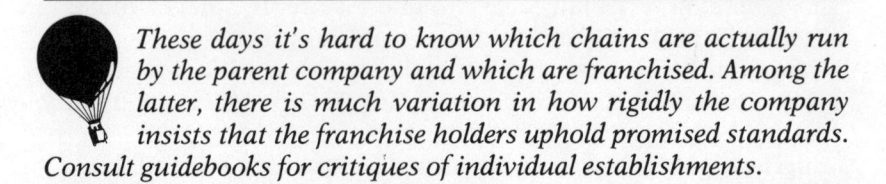

These days it's hard to know which chains are actually run by the parent company and which are franchised. Among the latter, there is much variation in how rigidly the company insists that the franchise holders uphold promised standards. Consult guidebooks for critiques of individual establishments.

Private hotels and motels. These lack the predictability of the chains—room arrangements, numbers and sizes of beds, and charges for children vary among private hotels and motels, and swimming pools and restaurants aren't always available—but independent establishments often offer unexpected charms. The rooms and the service may seem more homey than hotel-like, or there may be features not found in the typical chain hotel. How about a small private garden? A tea room? An oversized bathtub? Or a canopy bed? Just check ahead to make sure that you like what the place has and that it doesn't lack something you can't do without.

In some European countries, ancient castles, palaces, and manor houses have been converted into hotels. Some of these proudly claim to be haunted. Loaded with atmosphere, they range from moderately priced to expensive.

Private hotels abroad can provide very pleasant surroundings for less money. Accommodations vary, reflecting differences in culture. You can stay in a hotel in Mexico that has hot water only in the mornings; in Germany, you may have a sink in your room but have to go down the hall for a bathtub or toilet. In Japan, why not choose a traditional inn where you sleep Japanese-style on a futon on the floor? *Vive la différence!*

Resort hotels. For most of their patrons, resort hotels are a vacation destination rather than a place to stop over, but they can also provide a welcome break in the middle of an otherwise demanding trip. For information on resort hotels, see Chapter 8.

Special accommodations in hotels and motels. Some hotels and motels offer alternatives to the standard single, double, and twin rooms.

An American hotel or motel may offer a *suite*, which usually means a living room with one or more bedrooms attached. The living room sofa may convert into a double bed, providing plenty of room for a family of four even with only one bedroom. Suites can be expensive, however. If you need more than one room, you might ask if a special rate is available for *adjoining rooms*, two bedrooms that connect by a door (sometimes two adjoining bedrooms are also called a suite, or mini-suite). The hotel may be willing to strike a deal, especially if business is slow.

Some hotels and motels both in the United States and abroad offer efficiencies, family rooms, or apartments.

An *efficiency* is one room or a suite with some kitchen facilities—a small refrigerator and a sink tucked away in the corner, or a kitchen area with stove, utensils, and the like.

A *family room* can vary from one very large room with three or more beds to an average-size room with a small children's bedroom attached.

Some hotels are made up of complete little *apartments*. A kitchen, living room, and one or more bedrooms may provide the convenience of home along with the maid service of a hotel. You may find such hotels in large cities such as Washington, DC, where there is a lot of turnover in the population; new residents stay in these apartments while looking for more permanent homes.

> *For comfort and economy for the family of four, a double room with two double or queen-size beds, at a place where kids stay free, is often the most attractive choice.*

What to find out. Here are some things you may want to check when choosing a hotel or motel, whether you are consulting your guidebook or talking to the reservations agent.

How is the hotel rated? In countries where the government regulates hotels, the hotel's rating may help you know what level of services, luxury, and prices to expect. But in some countries the ratings reflect only the size of the establishment. Learn what the ratings really measure in the country in question. Some of the guidebooks available from bookstores and auto clubs also rate lodgings, according to the publishers' own criteria.

What will your stay cost? To answer this question, you may want to ask several others:

- What does the room price include? In foreign countries, room rates may be strictly regulated by the government or by a hoteliers' association. Prices will include all taxes and "service" (that is, major tips). In these countries, room rates must be prominently posted in the room, usually on the back of the door. There is no such regulation in the United States. The posting of rates in the room is required in some states, but the quoted rate

is likely to exclude taxes and service (though more domestic establishments are now posting all charges).
- Do rates differ depending on the size, furnishings, or location of the room? All the doubles may not cost the same amount.
- Are there special rates for children, or can they stay in your room at no extra charge? (In Europe, children sometimes pay the same rate as adults.)
- Are there lower rates if you stay a certain number of nights or during the hotel's slow time of the week? A motel that relies on weekend pleasure seekers may welcome your midweek sojourn with reduced rates, and "businessmen's hotels" in large cities may be half empty on weekends.
- Are meal plans offered? The "American Plan" (called "full pension" in Europe) includes all meals; the "Modified American Plan" ("half-pension" or "demipension") gives you two meals, usually breakfast and dinner; "European Plan" ("without pension") means go find your own food. Some room rates include a "continental breakfast"—juice or fruit; coffee, tea, or milk; and a roll or danish pastry. Hotels in some foreign countries always provide a full, hearty breakfast at no extra cost.
- If the hotel is in a resort area, is there a package plan that includes recreational features like greens fees, ski equipment, and the like?
- Are there any special promotional or low-season rates? Look for special deals intended to attract new patrons.

Exactly where is the hotel or motel situated? A hotel whose brochure says it's on the beach may turn out to be at the edge of a cliff overlooking same; guests may have a beautiful view and a hefty hike to go swimming. A hotel at the edge of a very large city could be forty-five minutes by bus from the part of town where many of the attractions are—if you can even get to a bus, that is. You'll want to stay as close as your budget permits to the places you'll want to visit. If you must do a lot of cross-city traveling and won't have a car, make sure that your hotel is close enough to public transportation that you and your kids can easily walk to the stop.

Where is your room? There's nothing like trying to relax quietly in your room, hoping the kids will fall asleep, while a clanking elevator keeps shattering the calm. A view of the trash dumpster instead of the bay can also be an annoyance. Again, prices may vary depending on where in the building the room is.

What special amenities are offered?

- Are nonsmoking rooms available?
- Is there an indoor or outdoor swimming pool, an exercise room, or other recreational facilities? How convenient is it to use them, and must you pay extra? Which ones are children permitted to use?
- Is there a babysitting service or nursery? Ask how the hotel gets sitters, whether they are bonded, and how well they are known by the establishment. Find out the nursery hours, who supervises, and what ages of children are accepted.
- Are there organized programs or structured activities for children?
- What kinds of restaurants or snack bars are there? Is room service available?
- Are there refrigerators in the rooms?
- Does the establishment offer free transportation from the airport to the premises?
- Is a concierge or other person available to find out about public events and get you tickets for them?

When you stop for the night at a hotel or motel about which you know nothing, you can not only ask about rates and amenities, but you can see your room before you pay for it. Even in expensive hotels this is a reasonable request. Test the beds; check out the bathroom. Ask to see another room if you don't like the location of the first.

How should you make reservations? Always reserve ahead if you know what day you'll arrive. The busier a city or area is likely to be, the farther ahead you should reserve.

In most places you will be expected to arrive by a certain time to claim your reservation. Four or six o' clock P.M. is typical in this country. If you arrive late and the hotel or motel is crowded, your room may have gone to someone else.

To avoid such a disaster, you can guarantee your reservation by prepaying for the first night or giving the establishment your credit-card number, so your room will be held for you even if you arrive late (still, you should always say if you know you'll be late). If you don't show up at all, of course, you will still pay for that first night.

Whether you guarantee your reservation or not, ask for a written confirmation to bring with you (a travel agent, if you're using one, will obtain this). By the way, when you guarantee your room you usually also guarantee the rate. Get that in writing as well.

If you must cancel a reservation, do so as far ahead as possible. If you have guaranteed your reservation, ask for a cancellation number and write it down. This will be your proof that you canceled the reservation should you inadvertently be billed for the room. (Be aware that some hotels charge a cancellation fee.)

Like their soulmates the airlines, crowded hotels and motels have been known to overbook. What if you arrive to find no room at the inn even though you've guaranteed payment? The hotel or motel may find you an equivalent room for the night in another hotel free of charge, pay for your transportation to that hotel, pay for a long-distance phone call to let your kith and kin know of the change, and pay to bring you back to the original hotel the next day, if you want to come back. You may want to ask in advance whether the establishment offers such compensation. If it doesn't do so routinely, and you're bumped, insist that something be done to make amends.

Ways to cut hotel and motel costs. A few tips can help cut the overall expense of staying in such places if your budget wants watching.

- The more expensive the hotel or motel, the more it will charge for its food. You might ask whether the establishment offers a package plan that includes some meals. Or take your meals away from the hotel; you may be able to breakfast at that pancake house two blocks away for half what you would pay at the hotel. Eating in inexpensive neighborhood restaurants off the tourist track can save you plenty. To find them, ask a few citizens, "Where do you eat?" (not "Where can we eat?").
- Although room service can be convenient (and a treat for the kids), don't use it if you want to save money. Keep a stock of snacks and drinks on hand, or bring something to your room from a coffee shop. Most hotels and motels provide free ice.
- Stay away from hotel shops, where you could pay significantly

more even for a tube of toothpaste than you would in a nearby drugstore. Do your souvenir shopping elsewhere.
- Stay in a hotel or motel some distance from the center of things but with easy access to efficient public transportation. If you'll have your own car, you can broaden the scope even further.
- Take a room without a view.
- Be careful about making long-distance phone calls; some hotels add ridiculous surcharges on to them. Ask before you call whether there will be an extra charge, and how much it will be. You may want to make your call from elsewhere.
- If you arrive without reservations and the room you're shown costs more than you wanted to spend, ask to see a less expensive one. No hotelier is going to show you the cheapest room first.

Inns, Guesthouses, and Bed-and-Breakfasts

There is a simpler world beyond the mass modernity of hotel and motel accommodations. Many travelers prefer smaller, more personal establishments.

Guesthouses are small, individually owned and operated hostelries. They may be in the heart of the business district over ground-floor shops, along country roads, or in residential parts of cities where there are no hotels. Some may feel like small, simple hotels, others like old-fashioned boarding houses. Your room may have its own bathroom or just a sink, or sink, toilet, and bathtub or shower may all be down the hall. Overseas there may be an extra charge for baths, in which case the proprietor or chambermaid draws your bath and provides a towel. Don't expect a restaurant in your guesthouse; when meals are provided, as they often are, the service is usually available to paying guests only. You will experience home cooking, at set mealtimes. Recreational facilities, if there are any, may consist of a sitting or TV room.

A variation on these small, personalized lodgings is the bed-and-breakfast, or B&B. Long popular in the British Isles, B&Bs have spread throughout the United States and elsewhere. They vary in size but are rarely more than a few guest rooms in a private home; you may find yourselves breakfasting with the host family in their kitchen.

B&Bs have traditionally been an economical choice of lodgings, but as the idea has caught on in the United States people have embellished B&Bs in both style and price. You can stay in a whaling captain's house in New Bedford, Massachusetts, or in the main house of a Southern plantation, if you are prepared to pay for the atmosphere. When inquiring about such a place, though, be sure to mention that you are traveling with your kids. Proprietors of B&Bs in historic houses furnished with antiques may prefer not to accept children.

In most parts of the world you can find farms that take paying guests. Staying at one is like staying at a bed-and-breakfast or guesthouse, with the added attraction that you can explore a working farm. A note of caution: If you stay on a farm where the milk comes from cow to table, you will probably be wise not to drink it.

Judging whether a B&B will suit your family may be easier in Europe than in the United States. European guesthouses and bed-and-breakfasts are rated and regulated by the national governments; these establishments must maintain specified standards, including cleanliness. But there is no such government intervention in the United States. Bed-and-breakfast associations provide directories of member establishments (see the Appendix), but it's hard to know what to expect without a guidebook. Fortunately, several guides to American B&Bs are available in bookstores. Local tourist offices and chambers of commerce are another source of information on local guesthouses and bed-and-breakfast places.

Staying in guesthouses and less expensive B&Bs can save the traveling family a good amount of money. But there is an even better reason to choose such lodgings. People who open the doors of their homes to others are usually quite outgoing and willing to share their knowledge. You and your family may come away with a heightened understanding of the region and its people, and even with some new friends.

Inns combine the small, personalized feeling of the guesthouse with the service of hotels and motels. Inns range from sumptuous to simple, and their character often reflects local culture and history. At an inn, you can immerse yourself in the spirit of colonial New England or the antebellum South. Kids take to such special accommodations at least as well as adults, and their understanding of local history and tradition may be enhanced by the surroundings.

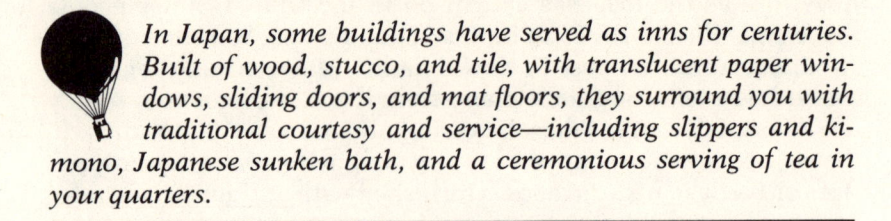

> *In Japan, some buildings have served as inns for centuries. Built of wood, stucco, and tile, with translucent paper windows, sliding doors, and mat floors, they surround you with traditional courtesy and service—including slippers and kimono, Japanese sunken bath, and a ceremonious serving of tea in your quarters.*

Most inns offer meals, at least breakfast and dinner. Unlike guesthouses, inns often open their dining rooms to the public, and many of them boast some of the finest regional dining in the land.

What to find out. Here are some questions to ask when you're choosing an inn, guesthouse, or B&B:

- Are any rooms especially suited for families? The rooms may vary greatly in size and arrangement.
- How much will your room cost? If your room has no private bath, is there an additional charge when you take a bath or shower?
- What are the rates for the kids? Children rarely will be allowed to stay for free in the room, but there may be a lower child's rate.
- Is a crib or cot available, if you want one? If so, must you pay extra for it?
- What meals come with the room? Are other meals available? Is there a child's rate for meals?
- At an inn, what special facilities are provided? Particularly in a recreational area, such things as bicycles, a swimming pool, and tennis court and equipment may be available.

> *The governments of Spain and Portugal sponsor national tourist inns (called* paradores *in Spain,* pousadas *in Portugal). Situated in former castles, palaces, or convents, or built especially for this program in areas of natural beauty, these inns offer first-class service at a moderate price.*

Last-Minute Room Hunting

Even if you've planned every day of your trip in detail, you may at some time arrive somewhere without a place to stay, perhaps because you've driven a greater or lesser distance that day than anticipated. Or you may have planned such flexibility into your schedule. How do you find a room at the last minute?

It helps to have on hand a list of a few possibilities you've learned of from guidebooks or a tourist office. Call or visit the hotels or guesthouses on your list to see if a suitable room is available, or go to the local tourist office if it hasn't yet closed for the night. Tell the clerk where you'd like to stay, and ask her to book a room there, or a similar room elsewhere. Or use the room reservation services provided at central railway stations and airports in some countries. The clerks there, too, can help you find a room and reserve it for you.

If a hotel or motel chain you like serves the areas you will be traveling through, bring along their directory and toll-free reservations number. The central booking office will be able to tell you what's available in each of their member establishments. If possible, make the call a day ahead or early in the day, as soon as you know you will need a reservation and can determine the most suitable location.

Should you arrive in a city during an event that has filled all the rooms in town, ask the tourist office to find you something outside the city. As a last resort, ask for a room in an expensive hotel or inn that the clerk may not have thought to call. If a room turns up, enjoy it! You'll probably make up for the expense another time.

Living Together in One Room

One of the most frequent worries we hear from would-be traveling parents is about how everyone will get along in close quarters. What do you do when the kids squabble and you can't send them up to their rooms? How do they get to sleep while you stay up in the same room? Do Mom and Dad have to swear an oath of silence, give up all their privacy, and content themselves with playing charades every night? Actually, with a little planning you can keep the tension down and the enjoyment up most of the time.

Although you may be able to arrange for a suite, adjoining rooms, or a large family room in the lodgings you choose, the most frequent arrangement for most of us is the double room—especially in the United States, where children can so often stay for free in the same room as their parents. Even abroad, and in the

United States when your kids are too old to stay with you for free, you'll generally pay less when you hole up together. So let's talk about how a family of four might manage in a typical double room with its two double beds. You can adjust accordingly if you have more room or more people to deal with.

Before we discuss anything else, we want to make a very important point about the physical arrangement of the room. Except for pieces that are affixed to the floor, *there is no reason that you have to leave the furniture arranged as you find it.* You might choose to move the kids' bed to a safer or quieter spot, or perhaps to clear one corner of the room to make a play area. Or you might want to shift some chairs or a table to give yourselves a place to read or watch TV at night so that the children won't wake up. (Before you leave, of course, you should put things back the way you found them.)

Getting the kids to sleep. Must you all go to sleep at the same time? Not if you don't want to. It's a matter of tactics. Give the kids the bed farthest from the bathroom. When their bedtime arrives, turn off all the room lights, leaving on the light in the bathroom. Go in the bathroom or sit in the doorway (pull the chairs over, if you like), and read, bathe, shave, polish your shoes, or do other quiet tasks while the children drift off. With you in the bathroom and the little ones in bed, the bathroom light doubles as reading lamp for you and nightlight for the kids. You can block excess light by closing yourselves into the bathroom or moving chairs around the bed.

Don't expect immediate results with this strategy, especially the first couple of times you try it. Staying in a hotel, motel, or guesthouse is exciting for the kids, so they may pop up to check on you, complaining that they can't sleep. Kindly but firmly, put them back in bed, and wait. This may try your patience, but once you've trained yourselves in the routine, single-room living can be a snap.

Unless the little ones are extremely light sleepers, once they are asleep you can come alive again. You will probably be able to turn on a lamp, chat, play chess or Scrabble, and even watch TV if you keep the sound low. If you have prepared a little area for yourselves away from their bed, you can while away a pleasurable evening. One of you might run out to bring back coffee or a midnight snack. We have even left babysitters to mind our kids as they slept in a hotel room, with much success.

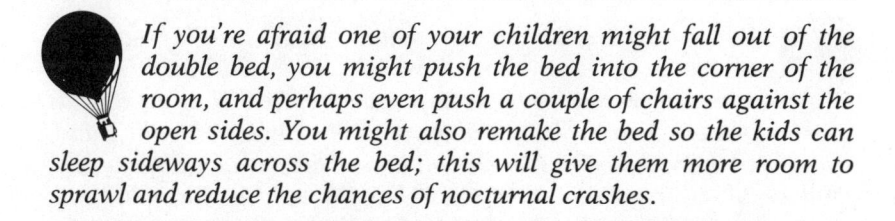

If you're afraid one of your children might fall out of the double bed, you might push the bed into the corner of the room, and perhaps even push a couple of chairs against the open sides. You might also remake the bed so the kids can sleep sideways across the bed; this will give them more room to sprawl and reduce the chances of nocturnal crashes.

Keeping your space from shrinking. If by the second day the room has become wall-to-wall clothing, toys, and food wrappers, it's going to begin to feel more like a multiple-inmate prison cell than a motel room. Try planning what will go where as soon as you've checked in. Place the kids' toy bags or suitcase in a corner with some play space. Once a day you can have a few minutes of cleanup time, when they put back into the suitcase what they aren't using. Designate a corner of the closet as the dirty-clothes pile. A plastic garbage bag tucked into the suitcase can serve as a hamper away from home. As little organization as this will reduce the clutter enough to make the room seem less claustrophobic.

If you think there's any chance that your child might wet the bed, pack a compact sheet of plastic or rubber to put under the hotel sheet. Many hotel managers are understandably nervous about this.

Ensuring peaceful coexistence. Get the kids out of the room to work off their restlessness. Just going down to the drugstore for a tube of toothpaste can provide a pleasant break and a chance to stretch the legs. A little walk around the neighborhood after dinner can relax everyone before you head back to the room to ready the children for bed.

Use the amenities: Consider having a meal sent to your room, just for a change of pace. Take the whole family to the swimming pool for some playful exercise, between outings or before dinner. Even that mushrooming menace to the world's quarter supply, the video game room, can prove useful when you're on vacation. If you don't allow much video game playing at home, permitting it on vacation can be a real treat for the kids.

Don't be afraid to ask for things not normally provided to

> When traveling abroad, we usually forget to bring—or plan not to bring—some items, which we instead buy in local stores. This provides a shopping adventure ("How do you say 'suntan lotion'?") and a souvenir supply of German Band-Aids, French toothpaste, or Greek shampoo. Items of clothing qualify; your child will remember "the straw hat I bought in Italy that hot, sunny day," or "my mittens from the Alps."

guests. Requesting an iron and ironing board, or a support board for your mattress, may get you only a surprised look, but you may be surprised yourself at how often such a request can be easily accommodated.

Snacks in the room can save you a trek out when between-meal hungries strike, pacify a child who wants to nibble, or make up for a dinner that was just too foreign for your little ones. Even in other countries, food stores will usually have more-or-less familiar snack items, which can be reassuring as well as filling for a young child. And having some nourishing munchies in the room can help save money, teeth, and general health by cutting down on trips to the junk-snack machines.

> We had been away from home with our two- and four-year-old for several weeks when we first decided to order room-service breakfast. They were both cartoon addicts at the time, so we planned a lazy Saturday morning in our room with the TV. Their enthusiasm for this idea took us completely aback; having breakfast in bed, in a hotel, while watching their favorite cartoons was a highlight of the trip for them. Even for us, breakfast in bed felt sinfully luxurious, and lounging away the morning rather than rushing off to see sights made for one of the most relaxing times of the trip. Ever since, we have tried to order room service at least once on every trip we take.

Once in a while, try to get out of the room without the kids. If you can't get a babysitter for the evening, you and your spouse can spell each other after the kids are asleep. While one of you watches TV or reads, the other can nip down to the coffee shop, take a stroll, or have a moonlight swim.

> *Wherever you stay, you may be able to arrange babysitting. Friends or relatives you're visiting may know local babysitters. If you're renting, the chamber of commerce, the visitors' center, or a real estate agent may have a list of babysitters.* Some hotels have bonded babysitters. Ask whoever refers you to a sitter how well they know the person and what reports they've received from other parents.

Renting or Swapping a House or Apartment

No other lodgings arrangement can match the ease of staying in a private, fully equipped house, apartment, or condominium. You'll probably have more living and sleeping space than you would in any hotel, motel, or guesthouse. And no matter how often you plan to eat out, there is nothing like having your own kitchen for providing quick snacks and early-morning bowls of cereal for the kids, or for satisfying late-night cravings. Renting a place may also mean you can enjoy the little extras not typical in a hotel room—a fireplace for those *après-ski* evenings, a sun deck and barbecue grill at the shore. If you take a place in a year-round residential area, you can immerse yourselves in the local culture by meeting the folks who live there; in foreign locales, especially, this can be a broadening experience for you and the kids. Finally, if you choose carefully, renting as well as swapping can be much cheaper than staying in a hotel. As long as you're willing to make your own bed and wash your own towels, renting a place to stay, or swapping homes with another family for a period of time, can be a great way to take a vacation.

Local real estate agencies are good places to look for short-term rentals; ask for some names from tourist offices or chambers of commerce, or look through the yellow pages of the out-of-town phone directories in your library. There are also agencies that specialize in short-term rentals and swaps; consult travel magazines, travel agents, and the Appendix for their names and addresses. Many of these agencies operate as clubs; an annual membership fee buys you a current directory of homes available, including pictures and descriptions. When and if you wish to offer your home, you send in your ad, but you don't always need to put your palace up for grabs to rent someone else's.

> *There is always some risk involved in house swapping. No matter how respectable the agency through which you make arrangements, you may come home to some things that weren't there when you left—a water ring on your coffee table, a broken washing machine. Compensation can often be worked out satisfactorily (and don't forget that your family may damage others' things, too) but you should decide—preferably ahead of time—how much such losses matter to you.*

Allow plenty of time to arrange a swap or rental. You may want to contact more than one agent to improve the chances of getting what you want. Be as specific as possible; houses and apartments come in all sizes and degrees of luxury.

What to find out. It is possible to rent a private villa complete with pool, tennis court, well-stocked bar and larder, maid service, and private beach. For most families, though, the important features are more basic:

- *Location.* The closer you are to the main local attractions, the more you will pay. The cost may be worth the benefits, especially if your children are old enough to have a certain measure of independence.
- *Number of beds and bedrooms.*
- *Quality of furnishings.* You may prefer a place that is relatively child-proof to one that is elegantly—that is, breakably—furnished.
- *Appliances.* Want a dishwasher? Clothes washer and dryer? Television?

> *In vacation areas, rental rates go down in the off-season; you might get more than you thought you could afford during summer in the Caribbean. Also, if you are planning a long stay, real estate agencies may have available rentals or sublets in residential as well as vacation areas. Any friend or acquaintance you have in the area may know of someone with just the place for you. Another good place to inquire is a local university or hospital. You may be able to land the home of a professor or doctor off on sabbatical or extended leave.*

- *Outdoor play space.* Is there a yard or a nearby play area for the kids?
- *Household provisions.* Are sheets, towels, and kitchen utensils provided?
- *Special needs.* If someone in your family is allergic, ask what pillows and quilts are stuffed with, or whether the owners have pets. The animals may not be there when you are, but their fur, dander, or fleas may be.

Camping

Toasting marshmallows over a campfire surrounded by tall pines can offer a sense of well-being unmatched by any stay in a luxury hotel. Kids love camping, and even very small babies do well sleeping out in tents; the cool night air seems to agree with them.

For most campers, cooking over a wood fire and sleeping in a tent (if not under the stars) are part of the fun of a camping vacation. But camping doesn't have to mean roughing it. Those who like to spend time outdoors but don't like making and breaking camp or shivering in a tent might want to consider renting a recreational vehicle (see Chapter 4). Even without an RV, you can enjoy America's wonderfully diverse state parks in relative luxury. Try staying in a Vermont park with three-walled rain shelters, in a cabin in the Virginia woods near a lake with paddle-boats, or in a yurt at an Oregon beach.

If you are considering tent camping for the first time, rent or borrow equipment and try your hand at it over a weekend or two before you invest time and money in a two-week outdoor adventure.

Although camping is attractive to people who'd rather commune with nature than socialize, staying in a popular campground is also a good way to meet other travelers, from different states and sometimes different countries.

Camping offers plenty of space for the kids to romp. You may, however, tire of the lack of space and privacy at night in a tent or camper. If the kids are old enough to sleep away from you, consider taking an extra pup tent or two.

In the United States, camping can serve as a way to enjoy the wilderness or as an inexpensive way to spend nights while you hike, swim, climb, boat, or tour the countryside. Most public and many private campgrounds in this country are in natural areas—near lakes and the seashore; in the mountains; in county, state, and national parks; and in national forests. Many private campgrounds are close to highways; a camping guide can help you find those convenient to your route. But few campgrounds of any sort are convenient to large U.S. cities, where a budget motel or B&B may be the best alternative for the economy-minded family.

U.S. campgrounds vary greatly in the amenities they offer. In some campgrounds, such as most of those in national forests, facilities are limited to picnic tables, fire pits, water faucets, and outhouses. Other campgrounds, usually private ones, have such facilities as swimming pools, stores, recreation rooms, and snack bars. Public campgrounds generally have larger and more natural sites, and many have hiking trails close by. National and state park campgrounds may offer nature talks by park rangers. Private campgrounds tend to offer less experience of the natural world and more conveniences such as hot showers. Most private campgrounds are a bit less expensive than state and national park campgrounds.

Give yourselves some extra (daylight) time to set up camp when you first go at it. The first time can be quite an adventure.

In Europe, where camping is one of the most popular forms of vacationing, it is generally less of a wilderness experience. Many European campgrounds have well-stocked stores, first-rate restaurants, laundromats, hairdressers, and even nightclubs. (You may see people setting up the most elaborate camps imaginable in these places.) In some European campgrounds you can rent a cottage or tent equipped with everything you will need other than your clothing and perhaps a sleeping bag. And because camping is so heavily relied on as a way to put up at night when traveling, campgrounds abroad are often located very close to, and at times within, major cities. You may be able to board the downtown bus at the campground gate and be in the center of the capital city in five minutes.

For a trip on which you'll stay in various campgrounds along your way, you'll probably want to get a campground directory, which lists facilities and costs for campgrounds of all sorts. You can find such directories in bookstores; automobile clubs and tourist offices also provide them (see the Appendix).

Before and during a camping trip, always assume it will rain.

Keeping Happy While Renting or Camping

While camping, renting, or swapping, you may have more space to spread out and a more relaxed atmosphere than you'd find in a hotel. But you must do without on-site restaurants, maids, and room service. Here are some guidelines for successful cohabitation in these circumstances:

Share the chores. You needn't split up housekeeping duties according to who does what at home. In fact, Mom's vacation could be made by having Dad or an older child take over primary responsibility for cooking.

Doing chores communally can make them go faster and more pleasantly for all. While Dad does the breakfast dishes, Mom can hang out the towels to dry, Jeremy can sweep out the tent, and little Emily can gather all the stuffed animals to put away before the family heads off on a hike. The Seven Dwarfs you may not be, but sharing the load can get your chores done efficiently, allow the kids to display competence and learn cooperation, and lessen the chances of anyone feeling resentful.

Allow yourselves a little luxury. Cooking, washing, and other housekeeping chores can seem like drudgery as the days go by. It can help to treat yourselves once in a while. Head into town to dine out one evening, and you'll feel cheery again frying up the bacon the next morning. Or bring in take-out food to your vacation cottage or campsite.

As when staying in a hotel, make full use of the amenities. Your rented or borrowed house may have features your own place lacks—a view of the sun setting over the ocean, a deck, a fireplace, cable TV. Your campground may have a swimming hole, hiking trails, even a museum. Enjoy these things!

When you're camping, you'll want to bring along some amenities of your own. "Roughing it" may be a lot more comfortable with pillows and air or foam mattresses.

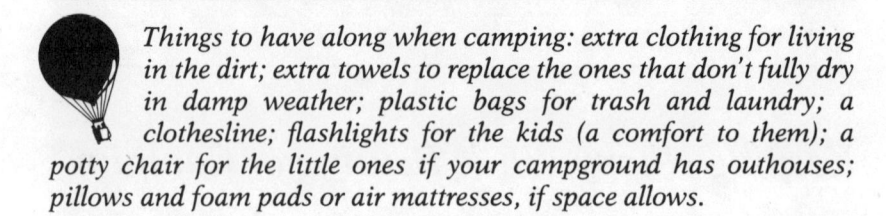

Things to have along when camping: extra clothing for living in the dirt; extra towels to replace the ones that don't fully dry in damp weather; plastic bags for trash and laundry; a clothesline; flashlights for the kids (a comfort to them); a potty chair for the little ones if your campground has outhouses; pillows and foam pads or air mattresses, if space allows.

Some extra tips for camping. If you're driving from home to the campground, pack digging toys and play cars and trucks. Your children may spend many a blissful hour building freeways and bypasses through your campsite.

Choose a campsite close enough to bathrooms and any playground that older kids will be able to walk there themselves and you'll have little distance to trek with your younger ones. But avoid camping too close to these or other noisy areas, such as beaches and camp stores.

When arranging sleeping bags in the tent, you and your spouse should put yourselves closest to the entrance, and instruct little ones to awaken you for nocturnal visits to the john. You don't want a half-asleep child wandering off in the wrong direction through the woods. Even if Katie is too sleepy to remember to wake you, if you sleep in front of the tent entrance you will undoubtedly spring to life when she steps on your face on her way out. And this arrangement makes it easy for you to scoot out if you need to without waking the kids.

Last thing before bed, march all the kids off to the bathroom. Then you can go to bed and hope.

A flashlight turned toward one corner of the tent wall makes a good nightlight when one is needed. For reading, you can buy handy little lamps that run on flashlight batteries. Whatever you do, don't use your gas lantern inside your tent or camper. Its fumes could asphyxiate you, and around children it could be a real fire hazard.

Be prepared for some early wake-up calls if you're camping with an infant or toddler. Your baby may wake up with the sun, see you sleeping beside him, squeal with delight . . . and squeal . . . and squeal. After a couple of nights he may sleep later, but turning in early yourselves the first few nights will help you deal with so much merriment at dawn.

Staying with Friends or Relatives

Whether the visit with your hosts is the purpose of your trip, or you just happen to know someone who lives where you want to vacation, your family should take certain things into consideration before deciding to be nonpaying guests.

Staying at a friend or relative's house is certainly cheaper than taking lodgings elsewhere. Your host may also provide more room for you to spread out in, companionship for your children, and even babysitting. Potential problems, of course, stem from these advantages. If your suitcases litter your friends' living room, your kids can't stand their kids, or your hosts begin to chafe at the disruption of their routine, your wonderfully inexpensive vacation may end up costing you a friendship.

Visits to close family members may have more lax rules. You may be able to follow more or less the habits you do at home, and feel you can impose a little more on the tolerance of your parents, brother, or sister. Still, consideration and courtesy is in order. Some day the shoe may be on the other foot.

If you'd really love to be invited back to your friend's wonderful house in San Francisco, follow two rules faithfully: Do the dishes, and leave before you want to.

Before you decide to take your family to stay with someone, talk to your would-be hosts about what tensions could come up. Make sure they really do have room for you—in their schedule as well as their house—and set a clear limit on your stay. Be realistic about your abilities to cope in these circumstances, and don't be afraid to decide that the arrangement won't work. You could spend as much time with your relatives or friends as you both like, but sleep in a nearby hotel or motel or in an RV in their driveway.

If you do decide to stay with friends or relatives, plan your activities much as you would for any other trip, assuming your hosts may or may not come along on outings, and allowing flexibility in case they've planned some activities for you. This is one kind of vacation that people often give too little thought to before they go. They assume that the hosts will have everything planned, or that they don't need to read up on their old hometown. By the third day of the visit, everyone is bored.

Actually, tourists often know more than most residents about what there is to do in an area. So be a tourist: Do your research and your itinerary planning, even if you'll be visiting your hometown. You may bring your hosts some unexpected pleasures as a result.

To be invited back . . . Learn the house rules and live by them. This means not only the obvious ones (no standing on the furniture) but also the unspoken ones you may not have at home, which means you must be sensitive to the moods and feelings of your hosts. If they have kids, let your kids follow their leads. If it isn't clear what is or is not allowed, by all means ask. And don't take for granted that you can spread out your family's belongings in their house.

If you have infants or toddlers with you, help your hosts by child-proofing a bit. Move safely out of reach those things that a normally inquisitive child of this age might get into: plants that can be tipped over or dug in, or breakable things.

When your kids need some running or loud time, take them to a park or playground, or even the backyard. Protect the peace of the house.

No matter how close you are to the people with whom you are staying, having a family with children as house guests can be wearing. Gestures of appreciation indicate your awareness of their effort. Get a babysitter and take your hosts out to dinner one night, or include their children on some special expedition, while their parents enjoy some time alone. Little gifts express your gratitude as well; staying with someone may give you just the idea for a small luxury that would make his life easier.

Don't let your hosts feel exploited. Bring home a few groceries from time to time. If you notice that milk is running low, stop while you're out and pick some up, or get some snacks, fruit, or cookies for their kids as well as yours. Do the dishes as they are used; read to their children along with your own.

> *If you and your children visit children of about the same age, you can swap your travel reading (comic books, for instance) with their hosts'. This may even work when the children aren't reading the same language.*

Don't expect your hosts to entertain you. Don't wait for them to plan activities, and don't feel that they must always come with you on outings. They may get tired of sightseeing; after all, they aren't on vacation, you are. They might also welcome some time away from your clan, and vice versa. Try to be sensitive to these feelings, and talk to your hosts about them instead of trying to guess what is on their minds.

Some Final Notes

Courtesy becomes even more important when you travel. Think about others when staying in any public hostelry. Your family might like to be up and out at seven in the morning, but hold down the chatter in the hallway as you pass the rooms of later sleepers. Sibling rivalry is normal, but a rip-roaring argument in the dining room ruins dinners other than yours.

On the other side of the coin, don't restrict your kids more than you need to. Our kids have had many a footrace down long hotel halls to see who could get to the room first. In the middle of the day in a clear hall with no one about, why not? Shouting in a dining room is out, but may be an inoffensive part of unbridled fun in an outdoor pool. Expect your kids to be courteous and considerate, but let them be kids.

Always have one parent act as a designated checker when leaving your room, campsite, or rented house for the last time. We recommended this once before for when you're leaving airport terminals, but here it's even more important. The longer you stay somewhere, the more you spread out, and the more likely you will leave something behind. Look under beds, through bedclothes, behind doors and draperies. This should be the very last thing you do before you leave, when all is packed (you hope) and the suitcases are sitting by the door.

You need not always leave as soon as you check out. Many places don't mind if you hang around awhile to use the facilities so long as you have vacated the room or campsite for the next guests. If you want to take one last swim or have lunch before heading off, ask if there is a place to leave your luggage, or to park your recreational vehicle. Do organize ahead of time if you will need to change clothes before you leave. Have a plastic bag for wet bathing suits and a change of clothes at hand for each person.

CHAPTER EIGHT
Family Resorts and Cruises

THIS CHAPTER DIDN'T APPEAR in the first edition of this book, because ten years ago there was nothing to say on the subject. Today things have changed: Through vacation programs designed specifically for families, you can laze in the Caribbean sun, explore the United States from Maine to Mexico, or ride the waves from Nova Scotia to the Netherlands Antilles. There are enough choices now that you can shop for the best features and prices, and it's a good bet that more and more of these services will become available.

Cruises and resorts are different from other vacations in one important respect: They provide food, accommodations, entertainment, and activities in one neat package. Although these vacations give you the option of exploring ports of call, or, in the case of resorts, nearby beaches, mountains, national parks, or other attractions, once you're on board or settled at the resort you can have a great time without ever leaving the premises.

Cruises and resorts are also relatively hassle-free. There aren't many decisions to be made other than what to have for dinner. Some resorts and just about all cruises are all-inclusive, which means that once you've pre-paid for the trip you can play, eat, and drink (though sometimes alcoholic beverages cost extra) without worrying about cost. And both cruise ships and resorts are terrific at pampering parents as well as kids. The freedom from decision making, the sense of being well cared for, and the presence of other families make all-inclusive vacations particularly attractive for single parents and for tired couples who just want to relax.

Choosing a Family Cruise or Resort

Newspapers and travel magazines often run articles on particular resorts and cruises that cater to families. After you've read up on some of your options, you can decide where to send for additional information. You may also want to chat with a travel agent who is well versed in family travel. If you describe what you're looking for in your vacation, a good agent should be able to present you with a range of options. (You'll need an agent, by the way, to book you passage on a cruise, though you yourself can arrange to stay at a resort.) Here are some factors to consider:

How committed to families is the ship or resort? Some ships with children's programs cater primarily to other clientele, and many self-described family resorts are merely large hotels with a lot of facilities and a few organized children's activities. Either of these may be fine for some families, but if you prefer a lot of potential playmates for your offspring, you may be better off looking for a resort or cruise for which families are the bread and butter.

Check the age groups for which programs are offered. A seaside resort that has one program for four- to eleven-year-olds and another for ages twelve and up either hasn't enough child guests to form groups with smaller age ranges or just isn't trying. But that New England mountain retreat with activities for preschoolers, others for five- to eight-year-olds, still others for nine- to twelve-year-olds, and so on, will likely have more facilities and staff for kids.

Ask what sorts of passengers make up most of the guest list. Different vessels draw different populations, which then give the ship a distinct character. Some attract primarily elders, others mostly young professionals, and some are definitely for families. You probably don't want your three- and five-year-olds to be the only kiddies splashing it up in that quiet pool where old folks swim slow laps. Resorts likewise vary in the age groups they primarily serve.

Are the programs and activities appropriate for your kids' ages and interests? A children's program can be pretty simple; perhaps a counselor watches your kids for a while in the pool, on the playground, or in the game room. Other programs are elaborate; your child may be able to spend as much time with the other kids and staff as she likes. There may be separate children's meals, slumber parties, and a stream of activities from dawn to yawn. Family cruises often feature kids' discos, karioke contests, scavenger hunts, crafts, pool games, soft-drink cocktail parties, story time, games, talent shows, ice cream feasts, and even walking cartoon characters, like Yogi Bear or Mickey Mouse. Resorts offer much of the same, and often add activities like children's tennis, sand castle contests, snorkeling and sailing classes, and trips to nearby attractions. Some have special theme programs, like circus training with a performance at the end of the week, or scuba programs leading to certification. Family camps may lack expensive entertainment and fancy facilities, but they provide fun activities in pleasant surroundings, and plenty of opportunity for socializing—kids with other kids, adults with other adults, and families with other families.

Many cruise ships have dress-up nights; check how dressy these are before you go. But don't overpack—closet space on board is limited.

If you're going on a cruise, find out if separate shore excursions are provided for the kids, or whether they must come along with you. On some boats the staff will even entertain the little ones on board while you're off searching Hamilton for the perfect pair of Bermuda shorts.

Are there activities or entertainment you'd like for yourself? Now that you're sure the kids will be taken care of morning, noon, and night, what would *you* like to do on your vacation? Cruise ships typically provide a wide array of possible activities, from reading or sunning on a quiet deck to visiting glitzy nightclubs and lounges with live entertainment, working out in an exercise room, and gambling in the ubiquitous casinos. Life on board doesn't differ hugely from ship to ship.

Very important, of course, may be where the ship will be going. Where are the stops, and what will they be like? Are there escorted tours to the Mayan ruins? Will you have sufficient time to browse in Phillipsburg for guavaberry liqueur? Will you be spending the day lounging on the beach at a posh resort?

Be aware of a potential shore-leave problem: The bigger the ship, the more likely that it will have to anchor off shore and unload the passengers by tender (that is, by a small boat)—a time-consuming process that will have to be reversed when it's time to reboard.

Resorts, of course, are more variable in the experiences offered. Ocean, mountains, golf and tennis, serenity amidst soaring pines, horseback riding amidst soaring cactus, Las Vegas–style entertainment with gourmet dining, campfires, barbecues, and nature hikes—any of these are available, depending on which resort you choose. The style and ambiance may be simple, extravagant, or somewhere in between.

You may want to ask whether babysitters are available to watch your children in your room or cabin. Persons employed just for the purpose, or waiters and waitresses, counselors, or other employees wanting to earn some extra money, are usually available to babysit at family resorts. Cruises usually give parents an evening off by feeding the kids as a group, then offering special kids' entertainment and perhaps a slumber party that lasts until the parents are ready to pick the children up. Some lines allow their employees to babysit for passengers in their cabins, but when this service is available the competition for it is fierce.

> *Since family resorts and cruises provide complete, hassle-free vacations with activities that appeal to many interests, they are good choices for multigenerational trips. Take along the grandparents as well as the kids.*

What are the mealtime arrangements? "Food, Glorious Food" should be the theme song of the cruise world. You can literally eat all day. This means flexibility and a lot of choice, and it's all included in the fare.

Lunch can be an a la carte meal in the restaurant, a buffet on the deck, poolside snacks, casual cafe grub, or a supervised children's meal. Pizza, burger, and ice cream snacks are available throughout the day, and who can go to bed without that lavish midnight buffet?

Dinnertime on board follows strict rules, though. There will most likely be an early and a late seating. Choose one and be on time. Your family will be assigned to a table for the duration of the cruise, perhaps with fellow passengers who will be your dining companions throughout the trip. Except when a supervised children's program is provided, the kids will dine with you.

Mealtimes at resorts run the gamut. Some resorts resemble cruises in that they offer many buffet-style meals. At a big resort, you could find yourself eating in a huge dining pavilion with two thousand of your closest friends. Another resort may have several restaurants to choose from, a la carte menus, and world-class cuisine. Supervised meals just for kids are more common at resorts than on cruises.

What are the accommodations like? Once again, resorts vary more than cruise ships in style and luxury. Some resorts offer family rooms that are larger and sleep more people than standard motel rooms; others have mini-suites designed for basic family needs and smaller pocketbooks. At a dude ranch you may stay in your own bunkhouse, at a family camp in a spartan cabin.

On cruise ships, you can find accommodations with sitting areas, balconies, or even suites—for a lot of money. Most families opt instead for the standard cabin. Expect it to be neat, pleasantly furnished, and small. There may be a double bed and a convertible sofa, or two singles that can come together to form a queen-size bed, with bunks that fold out of the wall. Some ships provide TV, VCR, and twenty-four-hour room service.

In selecting sleeping quarters aboard a boat you'll need to decide whether you want an inside or outside cabin. Inside cabins are less expensive but windowless. If you choose an outside cabin, try to determine whether it will provide a view of those Alaskan fjords or of a winch or stairwell. "Obstructed view" cabins are cheaper.

To avoid a noisy cabin, decline those located under the disco, show lounge, kitchen, or jogging track, or next to an air-conditioning ventilator or stewards' station.

What are the cost considerations? Choosing a truly all-inclusive resort or cruise can make budgeting easy, since all food, entertainment, and activities are included in the basic price. Find out, though, if everything you'll want is covered. Recreational equipment (scuba gear and golf clubs, for example) and alcoholic bever-

> *Cruise ship personnel are serious about passengers' being on time for the dinner seating. If you are more than fifteen minutes or so late you may not be admitted, so start getting the kids ready early.*

ages may be extra. Some children's programs may be included in the basic price, but others may not be. At many resorts, those pizza parties that keep the small fry occupied while their parents enjoy a quiet dinner are an extra (though usually worthwhile) expense.

Cruise lines charge according to the cabin's location, size, and amenities; the basic charge assumes double occupancy. Having additional persons costs extra, though the cost per person drops markedly when three, four, or five of you share a cabin.

The cost of a cruise often includes round-trip airfare to the point of embarkation, though you're free to arrange your own air travel and deduct the allotted amount from your tariff. Figure the costs both ways to see which works best for you.

On a cruise, plan to spend extra money for shore excursions, gambling, alcohol, souvenirs, babysitting, and tipping.

What if the kids balk at the supervised activities? Before the trip, talk with your children about what the kids' program will be like. But don't be surprised if they hesitate to join in the activities after you arrive at the resort or embark on your cruise. You may have to accompany them at first to help with the transition. If the kids' program provides an orientation get-together, take your kids to it. This will allow you all to meet the counselors, see the facilities, and obtain a list of activities and events. When you leave your kids in the counselors' care, let the children know they can rejoin you when they've had enough. Over a period of days, they will probably become increasingly comfortable in the group, and spend longer periods of time away from you.

Teenagers may be less interested in organized activities. After a while they may prefer to form their own circles of friends and make their own plans. In doing so, they will have achieved the same thing that the official program is intended for. And since they will be hanging out in safe surroundings, you won't have to worry about them getting into trouble. Going on a cruise or staying at a resort, in fact, can be an excellent vacation for families with adolescents who hanker for more independence.

CHAPTER NINE

Traveling as a Single Parent

ANGELA RARELY TRAVELED during her marriage. It was therefore with some trepidation that she planned the first vacation for herself and her two sons after the divorce. The drive down the California coast to a rented beach cottage was only a couple of hours. But Angela decided to spend a few nights there for a particular reason: She believed that travel would be one way to build a new life for her "new" family. And so it was. That first simple trip led to bolder and more far-flung adventures as Angela and the boys explored the world and their own interrelationships.

After losing his wife to a fatal illness, Don looked for ways to remind himself and the three kids that they were still a family. That search led to their first vacation at a family camp. The combination of vigorous physical activities, communal meals with other families, and relaxed camaraderie became a cherished part of their summers for years afterward.

Whatever your reason to travel with the tribe as a single parent, you are not alone. Since half of U.S. marriages end in divorce, single parents and their kids are becoming quite numerous among travelers. The travel industry has not yet responded to this trend in any significant way, but remember that just a decade ago there were very few travel services specifically for families; look how *that* has changed. With estimates that by the year 2000 the *majority* of U.S. children will spend part of their childhoods in single-parent homes, you can bet that the unmarried parent will benefit from future developments in travel, as will the married parent who travels with kids but sans spouse.

Most of the advice in this book is as useful to single parents as to couples. But because the solo dad or mom must shoulder full responsibility for the success of a trip with children, he or she needs to be especially conscientious about planning.

The Benefits of Single-Parent Travel

Trips alone with your kids can enhance your life in these ways:

Planning a trip increases interaction among family members. You'll talk and anticipate together, focusing on mutual interests. You may spend evenings poring over maps, reading brochures, and negotiating over how much time you'll spend hiking and how much you'll reserve for playing in pools and game rooms and meeting other kids. Such lively interaction will continue through the trip and spread to other areas of family life.

Traveling together strengthens the parent-child relationship. This is true of all family travel, but the effect is heightened when only one adult is present. You and your teenage son may share a sense of satisfaction after covering hundreds of miles of new territory with you driving and him navigating. You and your nine-year-old may share a moment of intimacy as you gaze with awe at the Grand Canyon. Such experiences increase feelings of closeness between parent and child.

Traveling together helps a newly defined family come together. If you've recently been through a divorce or suffered the death of your spouse, you and your kids may feel changed, not the family you were. You need to redefine yourselves. Travel can help you do this, in these ways:

- *Boundaries will be redefined.* In new and strange places, you may find yourself relaxing your parental role a bit. You and the kids may together make decisions—for example, to spend an extra day in DC to catch the Air and Space Museum—in a more fluid way. You and they may act more as equals, as you play together on the beach or snack in a sidewalk cafe on the Champs Élysées. And, when that restaurant you so looked forward to is closed, your children may find they can play the role of comforter.

- *The more carefree side of the relationship will come out.* Away from the chores and out of your role as supervisor, you may giggle with the kids at the taffy-pulling machines on the boardwalk, or laugh out loud at the antics of the Muppets at MGM Studios. Out of this shared pleasure will develop a new camaraderie.
- *You will see the kids differently.* Since nothing is routine when you travel, you may be impressed with abilities you didn't know your children had. You may admire the tenacity of your six-year-old as she struggles to finish a hike, or delight at your adolescent's flowering social skills when he shows up at the beach cottage with a new friend.

Traveling helps newly single parents feel better about themselves. Following a divorce or the death of a spouse, you may feel uncertain about your ability to manage for yourself and your children. Traveling can help you feel as though your life is expanding rather than shrinking. It can help you develop confidence; planning and executing a car trip through Canada's Atlantic provinces really adds to one's sense of competence. Travel can also help you learn to be flexible in caring for yourself and your children. Knowing you can cope when your rental car isn't ready for you, when the much anticipated amusement park has closed down, or when it rains at the beach can reassure you that you can cope with almost anything. Finally, travel can teach you to be patient with yourself. When you're trying to master the London underground or make do with your high-school Spanish, you can't expect immediate perfection. Knowing this may help you to loosen up a bit at home.

Traveling as a single parent has practical benefits. With only one grown-up along, travel can be cheaper, since kids' expenses are usually lower than adults'. If your kids are young, you also have more freedom to choose where you go and how you go. You can share these decisions as your kids get older, and your relationship will benefit from this.

Special Concerns of the Single-Parent Traveler

You may feel your choice of destinations is limited. This is a very individual matter: You may feel most comfortable away from places that attract a lot of couples. Or you may shun large cities, which may seem too overwhelming without another adult to help. Perhaps you don't want to drive beyond a few hours' distance if there will be no one to share the driving. What's important is to go places that feel comfortable to you, remembering that your range of comfortable choices is likely to expand the more you travel.

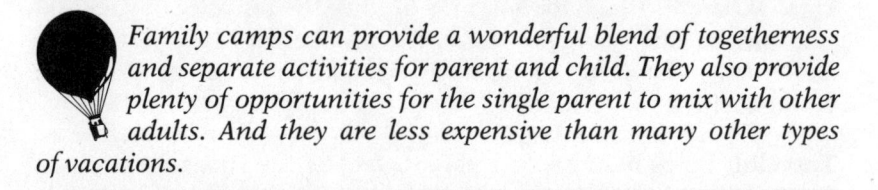

> *Family camps can provide a wonderful blend of togetherness and separate activities for parent and child. They also provide plenty of opportunities for the single parent to mix with other adults. And they are less expensive than many other types of vacations.*

There is no other adult to help. If your kids are young, the decisions are all yours. This can feel wonderful at some times, overwhelming at others. And when you're fatigued or feeling bad, having to deal with a child's illness, car trouble, or some other little crisis can be especially tough.

You may miss adult company. Aside from helping with the driving, decision making, and so on, another grown-up can be valuable just to chat with, especially if your children are young.

All of these concerns can be minimized with proper planning, as we'll show you.

Planning the Successful Single-Parent Vacation

All the advice we gave earlier about matching the trip to one's style and needs, doing research, and preparing an itinerary applies to the single parent as much as it does to the couple traveling with kids. In fact, as the only adult, you'll want to make your plans even more carefully, to reduce the need for decision making while you're away. Although it's still important to be flexible, increased structure will reduce anxiety while you travel and give you a feeling of greater control.

Go to places that feel comfortable. Familiar places and an easy pace will feel more comfortable if you're newly single. Head for that campground you know well, or spend a week lazing at the beach. A tour of the West Coast or a trip abroad will seem more manageable as you gain some experience as a single-parent traveler. Your first solo trip with the kids should be a beginning step in your new lifestyle, not a test.

Travel in ways that are comfortable for you. If you don't feel safe driving more than three hours from home, choose a destination within that range, or think about taking the train and leaving the driving to others while you enjoy the scenery with your little ones. Travel with another single parent and her children or bring along an adult companion. Arrange to meet family or friends along the way, if this will make things easier. Do preserve some time alone with your kids, though, so you and they can draw closer through your shared experiences.

Organize as much as you need to and more than you would if you were traveling with a second adult. Here's how one single mom plans a trip with her daughter: First, she lists the places they want to go and the things they'd like to do in each place. She then groups the activities by proximity to one another, and transfers the lists to a small daily planning calendar, which she takes along with her. Included in each full- or half-day block are the sights and activities of the place they'll be, restaurants that sound appealing in the area, and the name of the hotel where they'll be staying for the night. The calendar enables her to see a day's possibilities at a glance and quickly schedule each day's activities. Find your own organizational tools to suit your needs.

Make reservations ahead. In a busy tourist area or during high season, reserving ahead may save you from crankily scurrying around at the end of a tiring day looking for a room. Booking in advance may also be reassuring to your children, who could become unsettled by not knowing where you will be stopping. It's also nice for you to arrive somewhere at the end of a day's trek and have that welcoming person behind the desk recognize your name.

Talk with the kids about the trip. You can reduce unnecessary surprises, confusion, or uncertainty by letting them know before you leave home what you will be doing and seeing, and generally what you expect the vacation to be like. You'll probably do this more automatically with older children or adolescents as you share the decisions about where to go.

Plan driving trips with special care. Before you go, have the car thoroughly checked. Consider joining an auto club and even getting a cellular phone. Once you're on the road, you'll want to avoid overtaxing yourself and at the same time having to deal with an exhausted, whiny tot. So keep each day's drive short, allowing for breaks to stretch the legs, run off some steam, and take in a sight or activity to change the pace.

Look for guidebooks written for families. Slowly but surely, more of these are becoming available. They offer tips for things to do and see that appeal to kids as well as to parents. Also scout travel magazines, parent newspapers, and your newspaper's travel section for articles on places to go with children.

Remember that as the only parent traveling with small children, you will have to carry all the luggage. Pack accordingly.

On the Road, Just You and the Kids

You're off! These hints may help make your travels as a single parent as stress-free as possible.

Don't push your limits. This is so important that it bears repeating one more time: *Know your own and your children's limits, and respect them.* Don't drive for too long. Stop before the kids have fallen apart. Arrive at your destination early so you can unwind at the pool, in the playground, or in your room. Pay attention to transitions (the day of arrival or departure, for instance, or an airplane trip) and allow a lot of extra time to make them. Avoid anything that would stress you emotionally.

Stop at some places where you'll be likely to meet other adults. As we mentioned earlier, you might arrange in advance to meet friends or relatives and spend some time with them. You might also find adult companionship at a family resort. Small inns and guesthouses often provide opportunities to chat with fellow guests, and campgrounds are usually friendly places.

Have resource materials with you. Especially if you're going abroad, take along books and lists with information on medical services, local attractions, restaurants, automobile services, and whatever other travel needs you may have.

Go to fancier restaurants early. If you wish to eat in some more posh places, you will be better received before the evening crush begins. Your meal will seem more relaxed, and, if you worry about standing out as a single adult in such a setting, you'll probably feel it less at such times.

Take side trips in the middle of a stay. Let's say you and the small-fry have driven from San Francisco to spend a week with Aunt Ida in L.A., and you want to drive down to the San Diego Zoo for the day. Try to do this in the middle of the visit, when the trip will provide a change of pace and will less likely feel like *another day in the car!*

Allow yourself flexibility. You don't have to eat every meal in a restaurant. Sometimes, try picnicking by the side of the road or in your room, or order up room service just for the luxury of it. Likewise, if it's been raining throughout your canoe trip, don't feel bad about cutting it short. And if you are having a fabulous time somewhere, stay a day longer and lop something else off the itinerary.

Teach your older child how to navigate while you drive. This will help him to feel needed, and eventually make your driving easier (his navigating skill will improve with experience).

Money-Saving Tips

Single parents often need to travel cheap. Travel companies are just beginning to offer special deals for single adults with kids (some family cruises may offer you a discount). But these deals are few and hard to find. Always ask the travel agent, cruise line, resort, or hotel what's available to suit your needs.

Here are some other money-saving ideas:

- Eat a hearty breakfast and go lighter on lunch. Breakfast is typically the cheapest meal.
- Alternate a bed-and-breakfast or some other inexpensive accommodations with an upscale hotel that has a pool, game room, playground, and the like. This saves money while providing the kids with some entertainment and you with a bit of spoiling.
- Ask a travel agent to find you discount packages like hotel-and-car combinations or airline-and-hotel deals. It costs you nothing to use the agent's services.
- Research rental cars carefully. Be persistent in asking for less expensive rates. As with many travel purchases, the more you ask whether there is a less costly alternative, the more likely the agent is to come up with one.
- Go to busy non-tourist restaurants, where you can often find good food at reasonable prices. Overseas, this is an excellent way to find hearty peasant food and to dine with the locals rather than with Americans. Ask at your hotel for recommendations.
- Visit cities with a lot of free attractions. You could spend weeks in Washington, DC, without seeing everything and without spending for anything but your room and meals. Free or cheap attractions abound in most major cities; check the guidebooks.
- Use no-cost facilities. Enjoying lake or ocean beaches is often free; so are woodland strolls, mountain hikes, visits to city parks, and self-guided walking tours.
- Keep a cooler in the car for cheap lunches and handy snacks.
- Look for hotels and motels with refrigerators or kitchenettes in the rooms. They can save you a lot on food costs. In the absence of a refrigerator, bring your cooler into the room. Most hotels and motels provide free ice.
- Share a rented house with another single-parent family.

The great majority of single parents we interviewed told us that traveling alone with their kids has been an important growth experience, one that has given both them and their children confidence in themselves as individuals and as families. If you've been hesitant to travel alone with your children, these parents would advise you to grit your teeth, plan wisely, and give it a try!

CHAPTER TEN

Staying Healthy Away from Home

THE MATTER OF HEALTH can be worrisome when one anticipates travel to other lands. Are all those jokes about "Montezuma's Revenge" to be taken seriously? Is the water really unsafe to drink? You want to stay well, but you don't want to be neurotic about trying. For the traveling family, it's sometimes hard to know where to draw the line.

Before we had children we roamed the globe with reckless abandon. Those silly prohibitions weren't for us, but for middle-aged Americans obsessed with cleanliness. But just a few years later we were raising eyebrows all over Western Europe with the question "Is the milk pasteurized?" It's hard to say whether the change was attributable to our own aging or to the increased protectiveness we felt because we now had our children along. Were we too careless in the early days? Probably. Are we too cautious now? Who knows? For us, the rare occasion on which the milk was not pasteurized made up for the occasional silly feeling when the reply was, "Of course it's pasteurized! Where do you think you are, on the moon?"

In many countries you can buy whole milk in cartons that do not need to be refrigerated until they are opened. This milk tastes almost exactly like fresh whole milk, and is a godsend to pour over dry cereal in the hotel room for breakfast.

The more primitive the sanitary conditions and the more extreme the climate you'll be experiencing, the more cautious you should be. But the world is by and large not a threat to your health. In this chapter we wish to advise you of common travelers' health problems, ways to avoid these problems, and ways to deal with them when they occur. Often, the preparations you make to protect the health of your family in exotic places are not because those places are dirty, but because they are different enough to present your bodies with unaccustomed conditions. This is no reason to avoid those places. With a little information and some simple planning, you should be able to enjoy the wonders of this globe with your kids in good health.

Planning Ahead

How much medical planning and preparation you should do depends on where you're going, for how long, and what you will do there.

A visit to the dentist. A dental checkup is most useful if you're going to a foreign country or wilderness area, or if family members are cavity-prone. Make the visit far enough ahead to allow time to have any cavities filled.

A visit to the doctor. For a long or demanding trip, especially if you're going abroad, get a physical checkup. Discuss the demands that the trip will make, and be sure you're in shape enough to manage without great risk.

Ask the physician to suggest any medications to carry along for common problems like diarrhea, constipation, and colds, and when and how to use them. Ask when you should see a doctor about one of these ailments.

Refill any prescriptions for medicines that family members take routinely (such as for hay fever or asthma). Have enough to get you through the trip. You might take along an extra prescription, neatly typed, just in case. If you're taking habit-forming medications, you may need documentation by your physician to get you through customs without hassles.

Check that immunizations and booster shots for childhood diseases are up to date.

Immunizations for travel. Although shots aren't required to leave or return to the United States, you may need certain vaccinations to enter your destination country. The requirements change from time to time and country to country. Call the Centers for Disease Control and Prevention (CDC) International Travelers Hotline, 404-332-4559, for the latest information. Be sure to name all the countries you will visit, in the order in which you will do so; you may need a certain shot to go from one to another.

When immunizations are required to cross borders, the shots must be recorded on an approved form. These International Certificates of Vaccinations are available at passport offices, public health offices, and yellow-fever inoculation centers.

Requirements aside, you want to consider what is safest for you and your family. The CDC International Travelers Hotline can give you advice. If there has been a recent outbreak of polio somewhere on your route, for example, the CDC might recommend booster shots before departure even if you are all up to date.

If you travel to developing countries, vaccination against typhoid, cholera, or yellow fever may be recommended. Preventive drugs for malaria and other tropical diseases are often advised even if no government requires them. Make sure you understand the prescription; some malaria preventives must be taken before and after as well as during a trip. Also learn how else to avoid such diseases. Since malaria, for example, is transmitted by mosquito bite, your chances of contracting it are less if you cover your limbs, use insect repellent, and sleep under mosquito netting or stay in a place with good window screens or with air conditioners.

Should a family member become ill within six weeks or so following a foreign trip, be sure to mention the trip to your physician. This may assist in making the diagnosis.

Planning for medical help while away. Think about where you would go for help if medical problems should arise on your trip. If your destination is somewhere in the United States, ask your physician for the name of a doctor or medical facility there. If she doesn't know one, she will certainly be able to track one down.

You can usually feel assured of responsible treatment at a hospital emergency room in this country, though such services cost considerably more than private doctor visits. Even for problems that might not seem like emergencies yet want medical treatment, you can go to an emergency room.

If the language where you are heading is one you don't speak, a list of English-speaking doctors can provide a little security. Some automobile clubs and credit-card companies give out such lists. You can also consult one of the groups that exist solely to help travelers with their medical needs; we shall discuss them shortly. The nearest American embassy or consulate, too, can refer you to an English-speaking doctor.

Take some medical records with you. In your wallet, keep a list of any medications to which family members are allergic. If anyone in the family wears eyeglasses, keep the prescriptions handy, too. And if a family member has a chronic medical condition, ask your doctor to type up the important facts that another doctor would want to know about the history and treatment of the disorder. Know the generic names of any drugs regularly taken. You might use one of the medical record forms supplied by travelers' medical organizations, auto clubs, and some credit-card organizations.

Health insurance matters. Speak to your health insurance agent about whether you will need to pay medical expenses out of pocket, and receive any reimbursement on your return, or whether (in this country) you can authorize direct payment to the doctor or hospital and leave forms with them. In either case, if you do seek medical treatment while you are away, have the doctor or hospital give you a written statement describing the illness or injury, the diagnosis and treatment, any medications prescribed, and the costs. Make sure that it is signed by the attending doctor. This will serve as a record upon your return, either to submit to your insurance company for reimbursement or to refer to if things go awry when your insurance pays the doctor directly. If your health insurance is inadequate to cover your travel needs, think about getting a special policy to cover you all during the trip.

Travelers' medical organizations. These groups provide a range of health-related services to travelers. We shall describe two of these organizations; you can find their addresses in the Appendix.

The International Association for Medical Assistance to Travelers (IAMAT) is a nonprofit organization that depends upon donations. There is no fee for membership. IAMAT will provide a directory of English-speaking physicians abroad who the organization deems to have been trained to American standards. The foreign physicians who participate agree to abide by a schedule of payments set by IAMAT, thus protecting the traveler against fee gouging. IAMAT supplies medical record forms that you can fill out and carry with you, and pamphlets on such subjects as immunizations and malaria. The IAMAT booklet *24 World Climate Charts* (free if you donate $25 or more) describes climatic conditions, recommends clothing to wear, and assesses the safety of water, milk, and food in 1,440 major cities around the world.

For a per-person fee, Global Emergency Medical Services will provide you with a phone number of a local nurse who can assist you with medical problems or help you locate a qualified English-speaking doctor or clinic in the area. The organization will keep your medical records on file, to be sent if needed, and help you replace any lost eyeglasses or lost medication. It can even arrange transportation home should you become seriously ill, and provide a translator if needed when you're sick or injured abroad.

Avoiding Health Problems on Your Trip

Prevention really is the best medicine. Knowing what to expect in the way of health threats can help you figure out how to protect yourselves. And knowing how to respond to the little problems that come up can keep them from interfering with your enjoyment.

Exotic problems on exotic trips. More serious concerns arise the farther you stray from the relatively sanitized environment you are used to. In general, developing countries and tropical areas are where problems are most likely to arise. Even here, how vigilant you should be may depend on the part of a particular country you're visiting. If you're going to a fancy resort in the Caribbean, for instance, you may not need to worry about water or food, but you might be more cautious if you were off to rural parts of the same island. Consult your doctor and the Centers for Disease Control (404-332-4559) if you're going to a part of the world less traveled by Americans. And take these steps to keep the family safe:

Be careful where you swim. Freshwater lakes and rivers may contain parasites and unfamiliar germs. You may be wise to restrict swimming to filtered, chlorinated, and well-maintained pools. Oceans are safer than fresh water and poorly kept pools. Stick to beaches where the locals swim, unless the tourist office advises otherwise.

Be careful what you eat and drink. All food and water contains bacteria and other organisms, and in places far from home they will be different from those to which your body is accustomed. This can cause a variety of problems, such as upset stomach, diarrhea, cramps, and nausea. In some places, contaminants in water or food may cause serious medical disorders such as hepatitis or parasitic infections.

Where tap water is untreated, don't drink it, use it to brush your teeth, or accept it in the form of ice. Drink brand-name bottled water, familiar soft drinks, beer, or wine. Make sure that the bottle comes to you with its seal intact. If you must use the local water, boil it for ten minutes (take an immersion heater along) or add tincture of iodine or iodine tablets, which are available in drugstores and sporting goods stores. The Public Health Service advises using five drops of iodine per quart of water if it's clear, ten drops if the water is clouded. Let the water stand for thirty minutes. Chlorine tablets are also available, but they may be less effective than iodine. Also available in sporting goods stores are portable water purifiers, which give you clean water quickly and without the taste of iodine. Compact purifiers filter a cup of water at a time; slightly larger ones filter a liter at a time. Drink coffee or tea only if the water has been sufficiently boiled. Warn the kids not to swallow bath or shower water.

Avoid fresh milk and milk products like cheese unless they are pasteurized. If it's a long enough trip that the kids will miss their milk, take along some powdered milk which can be mixed with properly treated water. Packets of cocoa mix that need only the addition of boiled water can provide a nice change.

Look in outdoor or camping stores for a collapsible canteen that can hold a quart or two of purified water.

Buy fruits only with intact skins, and peel them yourself. Avoid fresh fruit juices. You can bring small cans of juice or packets of fruit-flavored drink mix from home if you feel you must have them. Eat vegetables only after they are washed and cooked.

In places without refrigeration, avoid salads and other cold dishes, dishes prepared ahead, mayonnaise, cream fillings, and custards.

Order your meat well done. Save your taste for rare steaks for parts of the world where tapeworm is not a concern.

If nearby ocean waters are polluted, be careful about seafoods, especially shellfish. Eat them only in the better restaurants, which may be more selective about where their seafoods come from. Hepatitis can be transmitted through shellfish.

Non-exotic problems in any location. You will all go off on your trip wearing the same bodies that you wear around the house. Avoid overextending them through grueling exercise, and give them routine care and maintenance. Vacations are times to relax the rules a bit, so go ahead and have dessert more often than you would at home, or stop once in a while for the kids' favorite junk food. But don't forget the nutrients, especially for the kids.

Adequate sleep is important, too. Be more flexible about the kids' bedtimes if you like, but make sure they get enough rest to match the active pace of kids on vacation. Bodies can resist illness better if they are well rested.

Despite all your precautions, little health problems may come up, just as they do at home. Here are some tips on dealing with them:

Motion sickness. Some children are prone to motion sickness; others have it once and it never recurs. A number of over-the-counter motion-sickness drugs are available for this problem, but you should talk with your doctor about their use, side effects, and suitability for the children. There are other ways to prevent or lessen motion sickness:

Heavy or spicy food or no food at all in the tummy can lead to or aggravate motion sickness, so eat a light meal before the trip. Wearing loose-fitting clothing can also help. Reading in motion can lead to nausea, so if your child gets motion sickness encourage other activities.

The back seat of a car is worse for carsickness than the front.

It seems to help if the kids can see out of a window (especially straight ahead), and good ventilation provides some relief, too.

Just being calm and sympathetic with your motion-sick child may help her feel a little better. Lying down helps some people, or try the old remedy of flat Coke or ginger ale to settle the stomach. Best of all is to stop for a rest break. Your child probably won't throw up, but be prepared with a plastic bag just in case.

Diarrhea. If someone in the family is prone to develop diarrhea, discuss this with your doctor. Understand how and when to use any medication the doctor might recommend and when to seek medical help.

The probability of developing diarrhea is greater on more exotic trips because of dietary differences and excitement as well as increased risk of infection. Whatever the cause of diarrhea, don't ignore it. Take a quiet day. The sufferer should rest, eat bland, easy-to-digest foods, and drink a lot of fluids to prevent dehydration. Clear liquids and soft drinks are useful; milk and very sweet, noncarbonated fruit drinks are not. Think about what you've been eating and whether moderation of something or other (rich foods, spices, sauces) might help. If other disease symptoms accompany the diarrhea, see a doctor.

Constipation. Consult your doctor before the trip if someone in the family tends to become constipated. Changing toilet habits can cause delayed bowel movements. Some people, including children, develop a regular bathroom time that becomes part of the daily routine at home. With all of the running around on vacation, the eliminative schedule may be disrupted. If someone in your family needs his usual fifteen minutes or half-hour in the bathroom to stay regular, plan this into the schedule.

As with diarrhea, check your diet. Grains, liquids, and dried fruits help relieve constipation, but stay away from too much tea, milk, or refined grains.

Jet lag. Also called *dysrhythmia* and *circadian desynchronization*, this is a condition in which your body's biological clock is out of sync with the time zone. Normal patterns of wakefulness, sleepiness, and other bodily functions are thrown off. Symptoms can include headache, nausea, dizziness, fatigue, insomnia, and lightheadedness. The more time zones you cross, the more pronounced jet lag may be.

Although there is no guaranteed preventive measure against jet lag, there are some things you can do to reduce its effects.

Begin the trip well rested. Eat sensibly before you leave, and dress comfortably. Help the kids to nap during the flight and to move around some for exercise. Eat and drink moderately on the plane. Watch especially the amount of alcohol you consume (too much can cause stomach upsets, headache, fatigue, and dehydration) and the amount of coffee or tea (too much can cause dehydration as well as jangled nerves and a shook-up stomach).

Allow some recovery time when you reach your destination. Take it easy the first day, and try to get yourselves to bed as near to your normal bedtime as possible—according to the clock on the wall, not the one in your body. This may not be easy; you may need more than one day to make the adjustment. If you've taken an overnight flight, slept little on board, and arrived during the day, you or the kids may need a daytime nap. Try to make it a short one so as to hasten adjustment to the new time zone. Eat simply and in moderate amounts the first day.

Pests. We use this term broadly to refer to animals, insects, or plants that might cause health problems, especially on outdoor expeditions. In New England, camping may involve biting black flies, mosquitoes, ticks, and poison ivy; in the desert Southwest, spiders and snakes. Scuba diving in tropical waters might bring you into contact with sharp coral, jellyfish, and the like.

As you research your trip ask your travel agent or tourist office what hazards to watch for or look for this information in a regional guidebook, first-aid book, or travel health book. Any of these sources may be able to tell you how to avoid problems and how to treat them when necessary.

Pest problems are more often minor than major. If you're not sure how to treat a problem, don't hesitate to go to the nearest emergency room or doctor's office. And don't feel foolish if the problem turns out to be inconsequential. The doctor may be pretty blasé about removing a tick from your son or daughter, but if you've never seen one before, it's better to be reassured than to ruin your vacation with worry.

Sunburn and heat exhaustion. On the beach, increase your time in the sun only gradually, day by day. Frequently apply sunscreen, with a rating of 15 or higher, or go out only in the morning or late afternoon. Cover up when you've had enough; fair-skinned children who burn easily may need to wear T-shirts over their swimming suits at all times. This is commonplace advice, but ignoring it can wreck a vacation. Ask your doctor what lotions are best for the kids. Some of them can irritate the skin, especially babies'.

In tropical and subtropical regions, consider the midday heat in planning your activities. You won't see the locals playing strenuous games in the middle of the day; they all take a rest break after lunch. Rather than running around in next to nothing, they're probably fully clothed, with hats. Follow their lead; go slow and protect your body, and especially your children's bodies. Drink plenty of liquids. If you're going somewhere hot and dry, ask your doctor about taking along salt tablets. Dizziness, headache, blurred vision, and sometimes nausea and vomiting may be signs that you've not protected yourself enough. Check with your physician about when to seek medical help.

The First-Aid Kit

An appropriate assortment of basic health supplies can go a long way toward quick relief from the annoying problems that may crop up. You can buy a first-aid kit at a camping or sporting goods store or at a drugstore, or make up your own. You might want to buy a kit that has most of what you'll want, then take out whatever you don't think you'll need and substitute other supplies. You'll then have the case to use over again for future trips. If you don't use a prepackaged kit, a small, zippered, plastic-lined bag or a hard plastic case will do for keeping everything together.

Keep basic first-aid supplies close at hand, in your pocketbook or another bag that you'll usually carry with you. If your first-aid kit is a larger, more complete one, you'll probably want to take out some of the things and put them into a smaller container for daily jaunts.

A very basic first-aid kit might include the following:

- aspirin, acetaminophen, or ibuprofen for adults; aspirin substitute for children
- antihistamine or other allergy medication
- antiseptic medication for cuts and burns
- insect repellent
- sunscreen

- ointment for insect bites and sunburn
- adhesive bandages
- premoistened towelettes
- tissues

For a longer or more adventurous trip, you'll want more first-aid supplies. Pack the larger kit in your suitcase if you're going by plane or train. If you're driving, you can keep the kit in the car. These items might be included in a fairly complete family medical kit:

- aspirin, acetaminophen, or ibuprofen for adults; aspirin substitute for children
- antihistamine or other allergy medication
- antiseptic medication for cuts and burns
- ointment for insect bites and sunburn
- ipecac, to induce vomiting in case of poisoning (consult a medical advisor before using it; some poisons require different treatments)
- medicine for diarrhea (children's and adults')
- remedies for constipation (children's and adults')
- medicine for motion sickness (children's and adults')
- antacid tablets
- decongestant (children's and adults')
- cough medicine (children's and adults')
- throat lozenges (children's and adults')
- vitamins
- antibiotics (if your doctor prescribes them for an emergency)
- petroleum jelly, for skin irritations and chapped lips
- antibiotic eye drops, for conjunctivitis (if your doctor prescribes them)
- oral thermometer
- small scissors, tweezers, and a needle (for splinter removal)
- adhesive bandages, gauze, and adhesive tape
- cotton balls or swabs
- antiseptic soap
- Moleskin, or Second Skin, for blisters
- water purification tablets or a water filter
- first-aid book
- list of English-speaking doctors (can be carried in the kit or separately)

This list presumes no ready access to the items en route. What you actually decide to include will depend on your destination, the physical condition of your family members, and your doctor's advice.

If you're bringing a baby along, you might add these articles to your first-aid kit:

- medication for diaper rash
- medication for the gums during teething
- rectal thermometer
- nasal aspirator
- decongestant or other medication you and your doctor think the baby might need

A final note about medicines: If a family member has a medical condition that may necessitate immediate access to medication, split up the amount you take between your pocketbook or carrying bag and a suitcase. This way, if a bag is lost or stolen you will still have some medication with you. You might also carry an extra prescription for the medication.

CHAPTER ELEVEN
Games for Traveling Families

AN ASSORTMENT OF GAMES is one of the handiest resources for the traveling parent—and it needn't add an ounce to your luggage. You may see your children getting restless when they have to wait in line or in a restaurant; you may hear the whine that means your toddler is feeling the wear and tear of a long day of sightseeing. Pulling the right game out of your bag of tricks could save the situation and head off a major crisis.

As you become more experienced at family travel, you'll be able to predict the situations that cause boredom, restlessness, or fatigue, and use games to prevent trouble before it starts. A collection of games can keep the kids from noticing how many hours they've been cooped up in the car, or how many miles they've walked.

You'll develop a feel for when to introduce a game; you don't need or want to entertain the children all the time. Suggest a quiet game or a more active one depending on the situation. And don't assume a game will be too simple or complicated for a particular child. You may be surprised at the ability of a younger child to understand a more complex game and at the power of a simpler game to entertain an older child. You can often adapt a game to make it harder or easier. Use your kids as a resource for games, too. It can be great fun for them to teach the rest of the family something new.

Quiet Games

These are most useful when physical activity is constrained and noise must be kept to a minimum—when you're waiting for your food in a restaurant, for example, or taking a long trip in a car, plane, or train, or waiting in a long line.

GUESSING GAMES

20 Questions. One person thinks of a person, place, or thing for everyone else to identify. The rest of the group ask about it, phrasing their questions so they can be answered "yes" or "no." They work as a team or as individuals to solve the mystery. If the family isn't playing as a team, whoever guesses the correct person, place, or thing is the winner. If no one guesses after twenty questions have been asked, the person who has stumped the others is declared the winner. The family can also divide into teams to compete against each other (younger children may prefer to be teamed with a parent). Take turns presenting the mystery to be solved.

I Am Thinking of Something. A variation of the above, this game can go on longer because there is no limit on the number of questions that can be asked. Again, only questions that can be answered "yes" or "no" are allowed.

The scope of both these games can be varied to suit the abilities of the children involved. With younger children, choose something visible (a picture on the wall, a fork, your waiter). With slightly older kids you can include objects, people, or places that are familiar to the family but not necessarily present (the children's bedroom, Grandma's cat). Subjects can become more distant as the children get older—famous people and places, and other things that are not personally known (the Eiffel Tower, a shark, Kermit the Frog). (When you play "Guess the Famous Person," the person who presents the mystery can start off by pantomiming some behavior the person was famous for.) It is best to begin with broad questions designed to eliminate categories (such as "Is it a person?") and ask increasingly narrow questions as you hone in on the target.

Guess My Rhyme. One person thinks of a word and says, "Guess my word. It rhymes with _____." The difficulty of the words can be varied to suit the ages of the children. The number of guesses can be limited or not.

COUNTING GAMES

These are most suited to riding in a car or train. Kids of all ages seem to like to find and count things as they ride along.

Find the Most. The point is to see who can count the most of something by the time you reach your destination or within a specified time limit. People choose different objects to count: green cars versus red cars, cows versus horses, pickup trucks versus trailer trucks. Older children might pit Buicks against Chevrolets or the license plates of two nearby states against each other. You might suggest that children draw the objects they remember or like the most when the counting part of the game is completed.

Find the Letters. Children look for letters of the alphabet in road signs as you travel along and shout them out as they see them. The object is to see who can spot all the letters of the alphabet first. They can jot each one down as they see it or start with the alphabet written out on a piece of paper and cross each one off as it's spotted. (To make the game easier, eliminate Q and Z, which are difficult to find.) If the children can read, they can also call out the word in which they see the letter. And, to increase the difficulty, you can have them find the letters in the order in which they occur in the alphabet.

RHYTHM GAMES

The Clapping Game. One player claps out the cadence of some well-known song (such as "She'll Be Comin' Round the Mountain," or "Baa, Baa, Black Sheep"). The others try to guess the song that is being clapped. The one who guesses gets to clap out the next song. This game can be enjoyed by young children as well as older ones. The chosen songs should be very familiar.

Categories. Here's a challenging game for older children. Players set up a rhythm by slapping their thighs twice, clapping twice, and snapping their fingers twice (once with each hand), in that order. The person chosen to go first (take turns doing so) begins by saying the word "category" in time with the rhythm, followed by the name of the category—fruit, flower, or color, for example. Starting with the player on the leader's left, each player in turn must then deliver in rhythm, while all players continue to clap and snap, the name of something in the category. Any player who misses the cadence is out, and the next player names a new category. The game continues until only one player remains.

WORD GAMES

Geography. The first player begins by saying the name of a city, state, or country. Each person following must give a geographic name that begins with the last letter of the place immediately preceding. For example, the first person says "Chicago." The next might say, "Oklahoma," the next, "Austria," and so on. No name can be used more than once. A player is out of the game when he can't think of a suitable name. The last remaining player wins. You may need to set a time limit for thinking of names, especially in the latter stages of a game, when fresh names are harder to think of. For younger children you could substitute animal names for place names.

Sausages. This is a very funny word game that will appeal to the silly streak in travelers of all ages. For each round of the game, one person is designated "It." The other members of the group take turns asking questions of It, who must obey two simple rules—she must answer every question with the single word "sausages," and she must not laugh. If she laughs, the round is over and the next person becomes It.

The questions may take any form, for example, "What's your favorite thing to sprinkle over vanilla ice cream?" or "The Pilgrims undertook their dangerous voyage to the New World because back home in England they had been treated like what?" or "What should you say to a pretty girl if you want her to kiss you?"

Players who become expert at Sausages may add a further degree of difficulty by requiring that the person who is It not even smile.

Willy. This starts as a guessing game, with the person who's in the know introducing his friend Willy and telling what Willy likes or doesn't like. (Willy likes summer but not winter; he likes books but not reading or writing; he doesn't like pasta, but likes noodles and spaghetti; he wears mittens, not gloves; he doesn't go to Texas, but loves Mississippi and Chattanooga, Tennessee.) Once the other players figure out that Willy likes anything with a double letter, the game becomes an ongoing amusement that adds spice to your travels. (Would Willy like to order a bagel? No, he'd rather have a sweet roll.)

Don't Say It. The leader names a word that must not be said (such as "no"), then asks the other players questions designed to get them to say it. A player is out when he cannot answer a question without using the outlawed word. The last remaining player wins. As a variation, players can take turns asking each other questions to elicit the deadly word. Or, for children who can spell well, you can rule out a letter of the alphabet rather than a word, and players must not say any word that contains that letter.

Telephone. One person thinks up a message to be relayed throughout the family, and whispers it to the next person. Each one in turn passes it on until it reaches the last person, who pronounces the message aloud. No one can whisper the message more than once, in whole or in part, so each person must pass it on as she thinks she heard it. The humor of the game lies in how fractured the message becomes by the time it reaches the last member of the family.

IMAGINATION GAMES

What Could It Be. In this simple game, one person names a familiar object. Each person then attempts to overlook the real uses of that object and to think about what other uses it could have (for example, a needle could be a lightning rod for an elf's house; a caterpillar could be a bus for ants). A younger child might need to see the object, or a drawing of it, to stimulate his ideas.

Storytelling. Serial storytelling among family members provides an opportunity for each person to use some imagination at her own level. One person begins a story and continues until a crucial point (for instance, the hero is in danger and must react). At this point the next person takes over, continuing until a similar point, then stepping aside for the next yarn-spinner. Even young children can tell part of the story, though they might not come to a suspenseful stopping point. The game can be continued indefinitely or limited to a predetermined number of turns for each person.

MEMORY GAMES

I'm Going on a Trip (Version 1). The first player begins by saying "I'm going on a trip and I'm going to take a . . . ," ending with the name of an object, such as *suitcase*. The next person repeats the sentence exactly, and adds another item ("I'm going on a trip and I'm going to take a suitcase and a baseball"). Each player in turn subsequently repeats the sentence, including all the previously named objects in order and then adding a new one. A player is out of the game when he forgets an item or confuses the order. The last remaining player is the winner.

I'm Going on a Trip (Version 2). Again, the first person starts off, "I'm going on a trip and I'm going to take a . . . ," but instead of naming a thing she makes a face or gesture. The game runs as does the other version, with each player attempting to remember the series of faces and gestures in order. Imitated gestures needn't be exact, but close enough to indicate that they were remembered.

PENCIL AND PAPER GAMES

Make Something Out of This. Draw a numeral or letter of the alphabet on a piece of paper (or a paper placemat at a restaurant). Have the child create a picture out of it. This is fun for all kids, even the little ones who may just scribble around the letter or numeral. The game can also be reversed so that the child draws the letter or numeral and the parent must make something out of it.

Connect the Dots and **Coloring.** You can easily create your own connect-the-dots picture. Just envision what you want to draw and do so using dots instead of lines. Don't make the dots so close together that the shape of the object is instantly recognizable and the surprise is spoiled. Don't forget to number the dots so the child knows what order to follow. Add a few crayons and your kids will enjoy coloring in the picture after they've connected the dots.

Hangman. One person thinks of a word that the other player or players will try to guess one letter at a time. The person thinking of the word draws a line of dashes, one dash per letter, to indicate the number of letters in the word. He also draws a simple gallows from which to hang the victim if the word is not guessed correctly. The guessers ask if specific letters occur in the word ("Are there any *A*'s?"). If a named letter occurs in the word, the person who thought of the word fills in that letter over the appropriate dash. (If a letter appears more than once in the word, it must be put in each place where it belongs.) If the letter doesn't appear in the word, the player who chose the word gets to add another body part to the hanging figure—first, a circle for the head; second, a line for the trunk; third and fourth, lines for each arm; and, finally, lines for each leg. This allows six guesses per game; if you want to allow more guesses, adorn the hanging figure with shoes, a hat, even facial features. If the guessers can guess the word before the figure is complete, they win the game; if they're stumped, they lose.

Find the Words. One person presents the others with the name of a famous person or a short phrase. Each of the players writes down the name or phrase on a sheet of paper. The object of the game is to rearrange the letters to form as many other words as possible within a specified time limit (say, five minutes). The player with the most legitimate words when time is called wins.

Word Change. One player chooses two words (no proper names) that have the same number of letters but share none of them. The object of the game is for the other players to change the first word one letter at a time until it becomes the second word. After each change, the letters must still form a legitimate word. For example: Change *lot* to *pin*. The steps might be *lot-pot-pit-pin*. With long words, the game becomes very challenging.

CARD GAMES

War. This is the simplest of card games but it seems to hold the attention of players of all ages. Any number can participate, but War is one of the best two-player games. All the cards of the deck are dealt, in equal amounts to each player (someone will wind up with an extra if there are an odd number of players; that's okay). Players keep their cards in a pile, face down, in front of them. On each turn they simultaneously turn over the top card. The player with the highest card takes the others and adds them to her pile.

If two or more players turn up the same value card, a "war" takes place. The two players place the next three cards from the top of their decks face down over the warring cards, then they place another card face up. The high card takes the lot. In the rare event that they match again, the players repeat the process until someone wins the cards. The game continues until someone has all the cards in the deck.

This game sometimes goes on a long time without a winner. You can set a time limit, declaring the winner to be the player with the most cards at that point. Or you can mark each player's pile of cards and set them aside to resume play at another time, thus extending one game over a period of several days.

Old Maid. You can buy children's sets of special Old Maid cards, but a regular deck of cards works fine. Just choose one card to be the Old Maid (one of the queens, for example, with the other queens removed from the deck, or a joker). All the cards are shuffled and dealt to the players, who match up pairs of cards (eights, nines, and jacks, for example) and remove them from their hands (note that only two of a kind, not three of a kind, can be discarded). These pairs are set aside. Beginning with the dealer, each player holds his remaining cards, face in, to the player on his left, who selects one. If it matches a card he already has, he can form a pair, and set it with his other pairs. If he has no match, he adds the card to his hand. He then holds up his hand to the player to his left, who takes a card. Play continues in this way until all the cards in the deck have been paired and discarded except for the Old Maid.

There are several ways to score. The person left holding the Old Maid can simply be declared the loser; the rest win. Or the other players can count the number of pairs in their discard piles, and the highest number wins. Or you can play several rounds, keeping track of the scores for each round, and call the player with the highest cumulative score the winner. Small children may need help fanning their cards.

You can buy round holders designed to help young children fan their playing cards. These are especially helpful in the car.

Go Fish. The dealer deals seven cards to each player, then lays the remainder of the deck face down between the players. The object of the game is to make as many pairs of matching cards as possible. The player to the left of the dealer begins play by asking any other players for any card that will match one in her hand: "Do you have any jacks [tens, aces]?" If the questioned player has the card, he must give it to the questioner, who lays the pair aside and asks for any card from the same or any other player. If the questioned player does not have the requested card, he tells the questioner to "go fish!"—which is done by taking the top card from the stack in the middle. If the card she takes happens to be the one she had requested, she gets to ask again. Otherwise, play passes to the player on her left. Play continues in this manner until all the cards in the deck have been paired. The player with the most pairs is the winner. As with Old Maid, smaller children may need help fanning their cards.

Crazy Eights. The object of this game is to be the first to get rid of all your cards. The dealer deals eight cards, face down, to each player. She places the remaining cards face down in a stack in the center, takes the top card off the stack, and turns it face up to start a second stack. The first player to the left of the dealer selects from his hand a card of the same suit (hearts, clubs, diamonds, or spades) as the card facing up in the center *or* a card of the same value (such as a four or a king) *or* an eight of any suit. He places his card face up on top of the one in the center. If his card is an eight, the player announces any suit he chooses to be in play. If he cannot match the suit or value of the face-up card and has no eight, he takes the top card from the face-down stack, and adds this card to his hand, or to the face-up stack if he now has a match. Play passes to the next person to the left, who repeats the process, matching the suit or value of the face-up card or using an eight card and choosing a new suit. When the face-down pile is used up, the face-up pile is shuffled and placed face down, with the top card turned up as at the beginning of the game. Play continues until one person has no cards left; that person is the winner.

A LIMITED MOVEMENT GAME

Rock, Scissors, Paper. We place this game in its own category because it really doesn't fit anywhere else. It's a simple game that can entertain some children for a surprisingly long period of time.

Each of two players holds one hand behind his back; in unison they say, "Rock, scissors, paper." Upon completion of the last syllable players quickly and simultaneously thrust their hands out front, holding them in a way to represent rock, scissors, or paper. Paper is represented by the hand held flat, palm down; rock by a fist; scissors by the middle and index fingers held in a scissors-like V. The winner of each round is determined by these rules: Paper covers rock, rock breaks scissors, and scissors cut paper.

You can play this over and over again just for the fun of it, or you can keep track of how many times each player wins, then total the scores. Or the winner of the first round can move on to face another family member as challenger. In this variation, the player able to play against each of the others without being cut, broken, or covered is the winner.

By the way, if you play this game at the dinner table, make sure the players aren't seated across from each other. It's a great way to knock over water glasses.

Somewhat Active Games

The games in this category require a little more space and provide some physical movement for the kids. But they are still relatively controlled, and so are useful, say, while waiting in a line or at an airport terminal, when one parent can take the kids aside for a while; on a patch of grass outside your motel room or on the grounds of a museum, where noisy activities would disturb others; or any time during a trip when a child needs a break from whatever else you're doing.

SITTING DOWN GAMES

Nails for Sale. One player is the seller of nails. Other players sit in a circle of imaginary houses, waiting for the seller to come to their doors. Choosing any player she wishes, the seller pretends to knock at the door and says, "Nails for sale. Will you buy my nails?" The other player pretends to open the door and says, "No, thank you. I wish no nails today." The seller then attempts to get the other player to laugh by making faces or talking gibberish. No tickling or other touching is permitted. Each time the seller asks her question the other player must repeat the same answer, without laughing. The seller may stay with one player as long as she wishes or move from door to door. Any player who laughs while the seller is at his door becomes the nail seller.

Take a Trip Across the Country. One player is the tour conductor. The others sit in a row on the ground, or on the bottom step of a flight of stairs, facing the conductor. They are the travelers beginning their trip. The tour conductor holds a pebble, button, or similar small object, the "ticket," in one hand behind his back. He then holds both hands out toward the travelers, formed into fists. He asks one traveler to guess which hand holds the ticket. If the traveler guesses correctly, she moves one step up or to whatever point is chosen as the first stop of the trip. Each traveler is given a chance to guess. Once a traveler has moved to her first stop, a wrong guess results in a move back to her previous stop to look for her lost ticket. The first to reach the top step or the final destination becomes the next tour conductor. You can label the stops on the trip and the final destination with real or fanciful place names.

GAMES THAT REQUIRE MORE SPACE

These are relatively tame but require a bit more room to spread out.

May I. One person is chosen captain. The other players stand in a line facing her, about fifteen to twenty feet away. The captain tells the players when and how they may move forward. There are a number of standard "steps" that may be taken, or you can invent your own:

- *Giant step*. The biggest step a player can take without leaping.
- *Baby step*. The smallest step one can take, done by placing one foot just in front of the other so the heel of the forward foot touches the toe of the foot behind. Once this is completed, the rear foot may be moved up next to the other.
- *Umbrella step*. The player puts one hand on his hip and the other on his head, then jumps up and spins in the air, attempting to do so in the direction of the captain. After landing, the player may turn to face the captain.
- *Scissors step*. The player jumps forward twice, once with the feet apart, then with them together.
- *Jump step*. Jump forward once with the feet together.
- *Hop step*. Hop forward once on one foot.

- *Leap step.* The player leaps forward from one foot to the other (not to be confused with the giant step, which does not permit the player's feet to leave the ground).
- *Backward giant, baby, umbrella, scissors, jump, hop, or leap, step.* The same step done toward the rear, away from the captain.

Any time the captain gives an instruction (such as, "Rachel, take one giant step"), the player whom she has instructed must ask, "May I?" The captain may respond, "Yes, you may," in which case the step is carried out. Or she may reply, "No, you may not." In that case the captain may go on to another player or give the same player another command. Players may only carry out the instructions after they have asked, "May I?" and been given an affirmative reply. A player who moves without asking, "May I?" and getting a yes from the captain must go back to the starting point. The captain has total discretion as to what steps she can call for, how many of them, and from whom. Players can try to move up when the captain is preoccupied elsewhere. But they must go all the way back if the captain sees them in the act of moving. The first person to cross the imaginary line on which the captain stands is the winner and gets to be captain for the next game.

Statues. One player is the statue maker. He takes each player in turn by the hands and spins him around like a top, letting go while the player spins. That player freezes into a statue in whatever position she is when he stops spinning. When all players have been turned into statues, the statue maker tries to make them laugh or move without touching them. The first to laugh or move loses and becomes the next statue maker.

Red Light, Green Light. The captain stands with her back to the others, who line up twenty or thirty feet behind her. When she says, "Green light!" the others may move toward her at whatever speed they wish. But at any moment the captain may say, "Red light!" while turning to face them. Anyone the captain sees moving must go back to the starting line. The rules can be changed to allow the players to sneak ahead while the captain's back is turned, before she says, "Green light!" But in this case she is allowed to spin around *without* saying, "Red light!" to catch the "cheaters" without warning. The first person to reach the captain and tap her on the shoulder becomes the captain for the next game.

Simon Says. All players face the one chosen to be Simon. Simon calls out simple commands such as "Simon says clap your hands," "Simon says touch your finger to your nose," "Sit down." Each time he gives a command he carries out the action, or, to trick the players, some other action. When his command is preceded by the words *Simon says*, the other must follow it promptly, but a player who follows a command not preceded by *Simon says* is out, as is a player who does what Simon does (say, touch the nose) instead of what he says ("Simon says tap your head"). The last remaining player gets to be Simon for the next game.

Simon Says (Infant-style). Give the baby simple directions to follow: "Mommy says touch your nose." "Mommy says clap your hands." For older infants, give two or three commands together ("Mommy says touch your nose and touch your ear"). As the baby learns to speak she may want to give directions back, thus providing her own variation of the game.

IMITATION AND OPPOSITE GAMES

Follow the Leader. Very simply, every player must imitate the actions of the person designated as leader. In small spaces where the leader can't go careening all over the landscape, he can use body movements, faces, sounds, changes in gait, and so on. Play the game so that anyone who fails to imitate is out, or forget about winners and losers and use it as a fun way to march yourselves back to your hotel room.

Mirror Imitations. How about not following the leader? In this game the leader makes movements or gestures that must be imitated in the opposite. For instance when the leader points up, the others must point down; when she sits down, the others stand up; when she makes a fist, the others hold their hands open. Those who fail to do the opposite are out; the last remaining player wins.

ACTING GAMES

What Am I? A simple charade game, this is suitable for both younger and older kids. The leader chooses an animal or familiar object to be. The other players must guess what he is by asking questions ("What do you do?" "How do you work?" "How do you move?"). The leader acts out an answer to each question. The first person to guess what the leader is pretending to be gets to lead next. With older kids, you can make the game more difficult by choosing exotic beasts or more complicated inanimate objects.

Charades. This old party game is adaptable for players of all ages. Players take turns acting out various things for the other players to guess, from the very simple (animals, nursery rhyme characters) to the very complex (book titles, sayings). No questions are permitted, only guesses as to what is being acted out. When acting out titles and the like, the actor begins by making a gesture to indicate the source of the phrase (she might pretend to be reading to indicate a book title, or pretend to be orating to indicate a saying), then holds up fingers to indicate the number of words in it. She then proceeds to act out one word at a time, indicating again by holding up fingers which word in the sequence she is acting out. The first person to guess correctly gets to act next.

GAMES TO BE PLAYED WITH OBJECTS

Book Race. Define a starting and finish line. At a given signal, each contestant starts toward the finish while balancing a book on top of his head. If the book falls off, the person must stop and rebalance it before starting to walk again. The first to cross the finish line wins.

Balloon Toss. Batting a balloon from one person to the next, try to keep it in the air as long as possible. You might draw an imaginary line and play a volleyball-like game, in which a player scores each time the balloon touches the ground on the opponent's side. No matter how hard you hit a balloon, it doesn't travel far, so you can keep within a small space and not worry about hitting others. Buy sturdy balloons so they won't pop too easily, and inflate them as you need them.

Jump Rope. Count to see how many times in a row the child can clear the rope, taking turns to see who can do best. Have the children teach you their favorite jump-rope chants from the playground.

Jacks. In this time-honored game, players take turns dropping a small rubber ball, trying to scoop up jacks that they have scattered on the floor, then attempting to catch the ball before it hits the floor a second time. Players begin by grabbing up one jack at a time ("onesies"), then two at a time ("twosies"), and so on. Older kids will know endless variations.

Active Games

Involving more movement and usually more noise, these games let the kids blow off steam. Save them for a trip to a playground or for the backyard of your rented vacation house.

TAGGING GAMES

Tag. There are a number of variations of this ageless classic. The basic game is often called *Touch Tag*. The player designated as "It" must touch one of the other players, all of whom try to stay away from It. A spot designated as home base serves as an island of safety where no one can be tagged. Anybody who is tagged while away from home base becomes It.

Shadow Tag is a variation in which It need not touch another player, but only step on her shadow to catch her. Obviously, a sunny spot is needed for this game.

Stoop Tag works like touch tag except that a player is safe from being tagged whenever he is in a stooping position. This position takes the place of a home base.

In *Spot Tag*, It must hold one hand on the spot on her body where she was tagged in the last round. This slows up It somewhat, so have some boundaries within which all players must stay.

All these forms of tag require three or more players, so unless you have a large family parental participation may be required.

RELAY RACES

Multiple Relay. A family of four or more can run relay races by splitting up into two teams. A starting line and goal are established. Then, on signal, the first member of each team runs to the goal and back, and tags the next team member. That person then traverses the same course, but in a different way. If the first person ran, the second might hop, skip, or run with his hands behind his back. The variations are endless, but both teams should agree on the order in advance. With only two people per team, the game can be lengthened by having each person take multiple turns. The first team to complete their turns wins.

Kick Relay. In this version of relay racing each person must kick something along as she runs. Use a ball, a stick, a can, whatever. It must be kicked across the goal line and back, where the next team member takes over. The game can be complicated by switching objects to be kicked (a ball for the first runners, a can for the second) or by varying kicking with balancing, bouncing, or carrying an object. For fewer than six players, you might want to extend the game by having each person run the course more than once.

GAMES TO BE PLAYED WITH BALLS

Hit the Coin. This game for two players requires a bouncing ball and a coin, bottle cap, or similar small object. The object is placed on level ground midway between the two contestants. Players take turns attempting to hit the object with the ball. There are two ways to score. First, each person can have a goal line just in front of the opponent; the object must be moved across the goal line to win. Second, a point can be awarded for each hit of the object (two points if it is flipped over), with the first player to accumulate a specified number of points declared the winner.

In the Soup. This game calls for three or more players. Two people stand some fifteen to twenty feet apart and toss a ball back and forth. A third person (or two people) stands in between, "in the soup." It is the job of whoever is in the soup to try to catch the ball, while those throwing try to keep it away from him. The middle person can move anywhere he wishes but may not grab the ball out of the hands of the others; he must catch it in the air or on the ground. When a person in the middle gets the ball, the person who threw it last goes in the soup.

A variation of this game can be played by two teams. Each team takes a turn attempting to throw the ball between team members while the other team tries to intercept. Everyone can move except the thrower. If a ball is intercepted, the teams switch roles. Points can be awarded each time a team completes a specified number of consecutive tosses without being intercepted.

Running Bases. You need three or more people to play this game. Two players stand at designated bases (a tree, a cloth, a bare patch on the ground). They throw a ball back and forth while one or more players attempts to run from one base to another without being tagged with the ball. The runners can be tagged only when they are not in contact with a base, and they must be tagged with the ball, held in the hand, not with a bare hand. Each runner gets three "outs" per turn. Players take turns running and throwing, and the one who "steals" the most bases wins.

Flinch. One player is chosen to be the leader. The others line up facing her, about ten feet away, with their arms at their sides. At her discretion, the leader throws a ball, or pretends to throw it, to various players. Her object is to get a player to flinch when the ball is not actually being thrown, or to drop it when trying to catch it. If a player does either, a point is scored against him. (The only time a player may flinch without penalty is when he is actually catching a thrown ball.) He is out when he has accumulated a certain number of points. A player who catches a ball becomes the leader, and the former leader takes his place in line. The game continues until only one player remains.

Sidewalk Tennis. This two-person game, played like tennis, requires a tennis ball or other bouncy ball. The players map out a "court," with a center line, end lines, and side lines. Two squares of a sidewalk are perfect; the line between them serves as the net. The ball is hit with the palm of the hand into the opponent's square. When a player fails to return a ball hit into her square or returns it outside of her opponent's square, her opponent gets a point. The winner of the point then serves the ball, and play continues. The first player to reach twenty-one points with a two-point lead wins. If the players are one point apart when twenty-one is reached, the game continues until one player gains a two-point advantage.

Kickball. This game is played like baseball, but with a large ball that players kick—an easier feat for young children than striking a small ball with a bat. Bases are set up as in baseball. The pitcher rolls the ball toward the kicker, who kicks it and runs to first base or beyond.

When playing with as few as two people per team, you can use "ghost runners." Suppose, for instance, that in a two-player-per-team game the first kicker kicks his way to first base. His teammate then kicks a single, sending the original kicker to second. It's the first kicker's turn at the plate again. In this case his place at second base is taken by a ghost runner, who can advance the same number of bases as the kicker for whom he's substituting. If the kicker makes it to first, the ghost runner ends up on third. If the kicker fails to reach first base, the ghost runner does not advance.

Score runs as in baseball, and play as many innings as you wish.

CHAPTER TWELVE

Family Travel ABCs

THIS FINAL CHAPTER is like the all-important pocketbook or backpack that accompanies you everywhere on your travels. It contains the essential items you don't want to lose sight of—in this case, the rather simple principles that can make a real difference in how much your family will enjoy your trip. Happy traveling!

ACCOMMODATING the needs of each person in your family as you travel involves advance planning. Adapt our suggestions to suit your particular needs, and be ready to adjust your plans as you go along.

BALANCE your plans so that kids and adults will both be happy. Do things everyone will enjoy, or intersperse activities geared for children with those that are more for adults.

CHANGE keeps people alert and interested; it increases curiosity and energizes the bored traveler. Even small changes (like who's paired up with whom) can help to keep the troops happy, if they're introduced at the right time.

DEDICATE some time each day for quiet rest and relaxation. Dawdle, dally, daydream a little. Don't push yourselves too hard.

ENJOY the fact that you have your children along. A Punch and Judy show could be an unexpected treat for you. Be a child again occasionally—you're on vacation!

FLEX-TIME built into your schedule allows for tired feet, hungry stomachs, and pretty flowers that simply must be sniffed. When planning your itinerary or a day's activities, think realistically about how much your family can do in a certain block of time . . . and then plan to do less.

GIVE the kids chances to not be on their best behavior; everybody needs a time and place to sag. It's also okay to help them out more than you would at home—a lightweight, collapsible stroller, for example, can be a godsend in city touring even if your four-year-old has long outgrown it otherwise.

HOW your kids perceive things will add immeasurably and unpredictably to your own experience of the trip. On the other side of the coin, don't assume kids can't appreciate "adult" experiences; share what's meaningful to you in terms that they can understand.

INDIVIDUAL family members need intervals alone in order to be able to cope with the increased "together time" on a family vacation.

JUGGLE your schedule to give each parent a break now and then. Just a little time away from Junior's demands can restore jangled, jaded nerves in a jiffy.

KEEP in mind that it's your vacation, too. Don't spend all your time coping with and entertaining the kids.

LEAVING the children with a babysitter can be as acceptable on vacation as it is at home, especially when your travels aren't demanding a lot of adjustment on the kids' part.

MAKE the few hours before you go out without the children a quiet time. Bring up pizza for them to eat in the room, or read aloud to them for a while before the sitter arrives; and then stick around long enough to ease the transition before you say goodbye.

NEW environments can require some adjustment time for most kids, so plan to get babysitters only in places you'll be staying for a number of days, and then schedule your evening out towards the end of your stay.

OFF-TIME for parents doesn't have to be away-time. For some, having the chance to read a magazine while the spouse plays cards with the children will be enough; others might need to physically remove themselves from the premises.

PSYCHOLOGICAL "space" is as important as physical space for a relaxing vacation. The expectation that every moment will be meaningful or fun, or the need to have everything go exactly as you imagined, can put you and the kids under unnecessary pressure.

QUALITY counts more than quantity where education is concerned. One baroque palace is quite enough of gilded splendor, and a quick visit to the best part of the museum can be fine. Don't take the guided tour unless your children are patient enough to hear all about it. Quit while you're ahead.

REGARDLESS of the ages of your children, they are going to perceive things and form impressions in a different way from yours. Rest assured that they will find their levels of enjoyment, excitement, and education; they will live every moment of this trip right beside you. Let them.

SHED your expectations about what everyone should get out of a trip. Relax enough to let everyone get what they will.

TIMING breaks for kids to relax and romp is more important than devoting a large part of each day to special children's activities. Be alert to signs of flagging enthusiasm, and deal with them promptly.

USE games and small activities to cope with static time, such as when you're waiting in a line or sitting at a restaurant table.

VWXYZ

Vacation time at last! **W**here, and **w**hen, and **w**hat, and **w**hy are settled; the **w**orld awaits you; you're on your **w**ay! We hope this book has **ex**panded your horizons; that the **ex**tra time and effort you've invested in your preparations will be rewarded; and that you'll be fl**ex**ible when the un**ex**pected occurs. **Y**ou and **y**our **y**oungsters can look forward to **y**ears of happy traveling, whether you visit **Z**urich or **Z**anzibar or feed the **z**ebras at the **z**oo in **Z**anesville!

APPENDIX

Automobile Associations and Clubs   157
Automobile Rental and Leasing Abroad   158
Recreational Vehicle Rental   158
Railroad Information   158
Camping Information   159
Bed-and-Breakfast Organizations   159
Cruises   160
Dude Ranches   160
Family Resorts   160
Budget Motel Chains   161
Home-Exchange and -Rental Organizations   161
Travel Bookstores   162
Government Publications   163
Travel Agencies   164
Passport Agencies   164
Department of State Travel Advisory   165
U.S. Embassies and Consulates Abroad   165
Medical Planning and Assistance   166

AUTOMOBILE ASSOCIATIONS AND CLUBS

Auto clubs offer travel information, reservation services, and other services to their members. Most are able to get an International Drivers Permit for a member. To find the nearest auto club, look in your phone directory or contact the main office of one of these two national organizations.

American Automobile Association
(AAA)
1000 Triple A Drive
Heathrow, Florida 32746

Mobile Auto Club
1130 Corporate Avenue
Lenexa, Kansas 66219
800-621-5581

AUTOMOBILE RENTAL AND LEASING ABROAD

Some of these companies also rent and lease recreational vehicles.

Auto Europe
27 Pearl Street
Portland, Maine 04112
800-223-5555

Avis Rent A Car System, Inc.
Worldwide Reservations Center
4500 South 129th East Avenue
Tulsa, Oklahoma 74134
800-331-1084

Europe by Car
1 Rockefeller Plaza
New York, New York 10020
   or
9000 Sunset Boulevard
Los Angeles, California 90069
800-223-1516, 800-637-9037
Within California: 800-252-9401
Within New York: 212-581-3040

Foremost Euro-Cars
5658 Sepulveda Boulevard, Suite 201
Van Nuys, California 91411
800-272-3299

Hertz Corporation
10401 N. Pennsylvania Avenue
Oklahoma City, Oklahoma 73120
Within the United States:
   800-654-3001
Within Canada: 800-263-0600

RECREATIONAL VEHICLE RENTAL

To find local rental companies, look in the yellow pages under "Recreational Vehicles" or "Motor Homes," or call one of the companies listed here. (To rent or lease an RV abroad, contact one of the companies listed under "Automobile Rental and Leasing Abroad.")

American Safari
National RV Rental System
11732 Annapolis Road, Suite 201
Glendale, Maryland 20769

Cruise America
11 West Hampton Avenue
Mesa, Arizona 85210
800-327-7799

RAILROAD INFORMATION

Tourist offices can usually provide information on national railroads. Following are additional sources of rail service information.

For the United States:
Amtrak Passenger Corporation
60 Massachusetts Avenue, NE
Washington, DC 20002
800-USA-RAIL
Or call a local Amtrak office.

For Britain:
BritRail Travel International
   National Railroad
Main Office
630 Third Avenue
New York, New York 10017
800-677-8585
Supplies the BritRail Pass.

For Europe:
DER Tours
9501 West Devon Avenue
Rosemont, Illinois 60018
800-782-2424
 or
Rail Europe
230 Westchester Avenue
White Plains, New York 10604
800-438-7245
 or
Rail Pass Express
7837 Sawbury Boulevard
Columbus, Ohio 43235
800-551-1941

For Japan:
Japan Railways Group
1 Rockefeller Plaza
New York, New York 10020
212-332-8686

CAMPING INFORMATION

Appalachian Mountain Club
5 Joy Street
Boston, Massachusetts 02108
617-523-0636
The AMC provides family camps as well as hiking and touring information, maps, and mountain huts for hikers.

Family Campers and RVers
4804 Transit Road, Building 2
Depew, New York 14043
800-245-9755; 716-668-6242
Formerly called the National Campers and Hikers Association, this organization provides the International Camping Carnet, an identification document helpful in registering at campgrounds abroad.

Recreational Equipment, Inc. (REI)
P.O. Box 1938
Sumner, Washington 98390
800-426-4840
This mail-order company carries Europa Camping and Caravaning, *a European campground directory.*

United States Government
 Printing Office
Superintendent of Documents
Washington, DC 20402
Send for Vacations Unlimited!, *a directory of U.S. national parks.*

BED-AND-BREAKFAST ORGANIZATIONS

These organizations provide listings of B&Bs and take reservations. Some provide these services free of charge; others require dues, or a small fee for a directory.

The Bed and Breakfast League, Ltd.
Sweet Dreams and Toast, Inc.
P.O. Box 9490
Washington, DC 20016
202-363-7767
A reservation service for B&Bs in and near Washington, DC.

Berkshire Bed and Breakfast Reservation Service
P.O. Box 711
Williamsburg, Massachusetts 01096
413-268-7244
For B&Bs in western Massachusetts and eastern New York.

Worldwide Bed and Breakfast Reservation Service
P.O. Box 14841
Baton Rouge, Louisiana 70898
504-336-4035
For B&Bs all over the world.

CRUISES

Cruise Lines International Association
500 Fifth Avenue, Suite 1407
New York, New York 10110
212-921-0066
Ask for Cruising—Answers to Your Questions, *a free pamphlet that lists cruise lines with children's programs and other amenities for families.*

DUDE RANCHES

Dude Ranchers Association
P.O. Box 471
LaPorte, Colorado 80535
303-223-8440
Provides a free directory of dude ranches, which also lists those with children's programs.

FAMILY RESORTS

Boscobel Beach (a SuperClubs Resort)
P.O. Box 63
Ocho Rios, Jamaica, West Indies
800-849-SUPER

Club Med
40 West 57th Street
New York, New York 10019
800-CLUB MED

Hyatt Hotels Corporation
(Camp Hyatt)
200 West Madison
Chicago, Illinois 60606
800-233-1234

Sonesta International Hotels
   Corporation
"JUST US KIDS" program
350 Ocean Drive
Key Biscayne, Florida 33149
800-SONESTA

BUDGET MOTEL CHAINS

Call for telephone numbers of motels in the area you'll be traveling through, or write for directories of motel locations, amenities, and prices.

Budget Host Inns
P.O. Box 12188
Arlington, Texas 76094
800-283-4678

Choice Hotels (Quality Inn,
   Comfort Inn, Sleep Inn, Econo
   Lodge, Rodeway Inn, and
   Friendship Inn)
10750 Columbia Pike
Silver Spring, Maryland 20901
800-424-6423, 800-221-2222

Days Inn
P.O. Box 29004
Phoenix, Arizona 85038
800-DAYS INN

Family Inns of America
P.O. Box 1298
Chamber of Commerce
Pigeon Forge, Tennessee 37868
800-221-9858

Motel 6
14651 Dallas Parkway, Suite 500
Dallas, Texas 75240
800-437-7486

Red Roof Inns
4355 Davidson Road
Hillard, Ohio 43026
800-843-7663

Suisse Chalet
2 Progress Avenue
Nashua, New Hampshire 03062
800-258-1980

Super 8 Motels
1910 Eighth Avenue, NE
Aberdeen, South Dakota 57401
800-800-8000

HOME-EXCHANGE AND -RENTAL ORGANIZATIONS

Home-exchange directories may include not only houses and apartments but also houseboats, yachts, and recreational vehicles available for rent or swap.

Hideaways International
767 Islington Street
Portsmouth, New Hampshire
   03801
800-843-4433

Home Exchange Unlimited
18547 Soledad Canyon Road,
   Suite 223
Santa Clarita, California 91351
805-251-1238

Homelink USA (Vacation
   Exchange Club)
P.O. Box 650
Key West, Florida 33041
800-638-3841

INTERVAC U.S.
International Home Exchange
P.O. Box 59054
San Francisco, California 94159
800-756-HOME

Villas International
605 Market Street, Suite 510
San Francisco, California 94105
800-221-2260

TRAVEL BOOKSTORES

All of these stores welcome both walk-in customers and telephone orders. Some of the stores offer mail-order catalogs; others will send newsletters about the books they stock.

California:
Book Passage
51 Tamal Vista
Corte Madera, California 94925
800-999-7909, 415-927-0960
Annual mail-order catalog; newsletter.
   or
Phileas Fogg's Books
87 Stanford Shopping Center
Palo Alto, California
800-533-FOGG, 415-327-1754
Newsletter.
   or
Traveler's Depot
1655 Garnet Avenue
San Diego, California 92109
619-483-1421
Newsletter.

Illinois:
Sandemeyer's
714 South Dearborn
Chicago, Illinois 60605
312-922-2104
   or
Savvy Traveler
310 South Michigan Avenue
Chicago, Illinois 60604
312-913-9800
Quarterly newsletter; geography and activity books for kids.

Kansas:
Forsyth Travel Library
9154 West 57th Street, Box 2975
Shawnee Mission, Kansas 66201
800-913-384-3440
Mail-order catalog.

Maryland:
Travel Books and Language
   Center, Inc.
4931 Cordell Avenue
Bethesda, Maryland 20814
800-220-2665, 301-951-8533

Massachusetts:
Globe Corner Bookstore
3 School Street
Boston, Massachusetts 02108
800-358-6013, 617-523-6658
Newsletter.

New York:
Complete Traveler Bookstore
199 Madison Avenue
New York, New York 10016
212-685-9007
Mail-order catalog.

Oregon:
Powell's Travel Bookstore
701 Southwest Sixth Avenue
Portland, Oregon 97204
800-546-5025, 503-228-1108

Washington:
Wide World Books and Maps
1911 North 45th Street
Seattle, Washington 98103
206-634-3453
Mail-order catalog.

GOVERNMENT PUBLICATIONS

Some of these publications are free; a small fee is charged for others. Write or call the listed agency for information.

Farm Vacations
Room 535A
U.S. Department of Agriculture
Washington, DC 20250

Foreign Entry Requirements and *Passports—Applying for Them the EASY WAY*
Consumer Information Center
Pueblo, Colorado 81009
These booklets are also available in regional passport offices (see page 164).

Know Before You Go: Customs Hints for Returning U.S. Residents
U.S. Customs Service
P.O. Box 7407
Washington, DC 20044
This booklet is also available from regional customs offices, which are situated in major U.S. cities.

Vacations Unlimited! (a guide to national parks), *Your Trip Abroad*, and *Health Information for International Travel*
United States Government Printing Office
Superintendent of Documents
Washington, DC 20402
202-783-3238

Visiting Indian Reservations
Bureau of Indian Affairs
1951 Constitution Avenue, NW
Washington, DC 20245

TRAVEL AGENCIES

The largest organization of travel agencies will hear your complaints about any member agency.

American Society of Travel Agents
  (ASTA)
Consumer Affairs Department
1101 King Street, Suite 200
Alexandria, Virginia 22314
703-739-2851

PASSPORT AGENCIES

For each office, two telephone numbers are listed. The first is a round-the-clock recording that provides general passport information, tells where the office is situated, and gives the hours of operation. The second phone number is for additional information. Passport applications are also available in many post offices.

Boston:
Thomas P. O'Neill Federal
  Building, Room 247
10 Causeway Street
Boston, Massachusetts 02222
Recording: 617-565-6998
Inquiries: 617-565-6990

Chicago:
Kluczynski Federal Building,
  Suite 380
230 South Dearborn
Chicago, Illinois 60604
Recording: 312-353-5426
Inquiries: 312-353-7155,
  312-353-7163

Honolulu:
New Federal Building, Room C-106
300 Ala Moana Boulevard
Honolulu, Hawaii 96850
Recording: 808-541-1919
Inquiries: 808-541-1918

Houston:
Mickey Leland Federal Building,
  Suite 1100
1919 Smith Street
Houston, Texas 77002
Recording: 713-653-3159
Inquiries: 713-653-3153

Los Angeles:
11000 Wilshire Boulevard, Room
  13100
Los Angeles, California 90024
Recording: 310-575-7070
Inquiries: 213-824-7075

Miami:
Federal Office Building, Third
  Floor
51 Southwest First Avenue
Miami, Florida 33130
Recording: 305-536-5395 (English),
  305-536-4448 (Spanish)
Inquiries: 305-536-4681

New Orleans:
Postal Services Building,
 Room T-12005
701 Loyola Avenue
New Orleans, Louisiana 70013
Recording: 504-589-6728
Inquiries: 504-589-6161

New York:
Rockefeller Center, Room 270
630 Fifth Avenue
New York, New York 10111
Recording: 212-541-7700
Inquiries: 212-541-7710

Philadelphia:
Federal Building, Room 4426
600 Arch Street
Philadelphia, Pennsylvania 19106
Recording: 215-597-7482
Inquiries: 215-597-7480

San Francisco:
Tishman Speyer Building, Suite 200
525 Market Street
San Francisco, California 94105
Recording: 415-744-4444
Inquiries: 415-744-4010

Seattle:
Federal Office Building, Room 992
915 Second Avenue
Seattle, Washington 98174
Recording: 206-553-7941
Inquiries: 206-553-7945

Stamford:
One Landmark Square
Broad and Atlantic Streets
Stamford, Connecticut 06901
Recording: 203-325-4401
Inquiries: 203-325-3538,
 203-325-3530

Washington:
1425 K Street, NW
Washington, DC 20524
Recording: 202-647-0518
Inquiries: 202-326-6020

DEPARTMENT OF STATE TRAVEL ADVISORY

For information on political or health problems in various countries, call 202-647-5225.

U.S. EMBASSIES AND CONSULATES ABROAD

Our embassies and consulates are official representatives of the U.S. government to the countries in which they are situated. They do assist U.S. citizens traveling in their host countries, but only as necessary to ensure safe conduct and provide emergency help. They cannot serve as travel agents; they will not cash your personal check; they won't receive mail for you; and they cannot exempt you from local laws.

But embassies and consulates do assist travelers in certain kinds of crises. They can provide lists of English-speaking doctors or lawyers. In a medical emergency they will inform the next of kin. In a legal crisis they will try to see that you are treated fairly, but will not and cannot interfere with the legal system of the host country. They can provide a loan (you must sign a promissory note) to get you home if you are stranded without funds. The money can be used only so you can return home immediately, not so you can continue your trip. Your passport, in fact, will be stamped "For direct return to the U.S. only" until the loan is repaid. Such a loan is only granted as a last resort, if you have exhausted all efforts to borrow money from friends or relatives at home. Embassies and consulates will issue a temporary passport to replace a lost or stolen one. They will provide aid and necessary evacuation in the event of civil unrest or natural disaster. They will help those at home locate missing family members overseas. Think of embassies and consulates as available to help in extraordinary circumstances, not as a convenience service for travelers.

To find the addresses and telephone numbers of embassies and consulates, call or write for this booklet:

Key Officers of Foreign Service Posts
Superintendent of Documents
U.S. Government Printing Office
Washington, DC 20402
202-783-3238

Or, after you reach your destination, ask at the local tourist office or police station or look in a big-city telephone directory.

MEDICAL PLANNING AND ASSISTANCE

Leonard C. Marcus VMD, MD
148 Highland Avenue
Newton, Massachusetts 02165
For a directory of physicians in the United States and Canada who specialize in travelers' health, send a self-addressed 8½-by-11-inch envelope with $1.01 postage.

Global Emergency Medical Services
2001 Westside Drive, Suite 120
Alpharetta, Georgia 30201
800-860-1111

International Association for Medical Assistance to Travelers (IAMAT)
417 Center Street
Lewiston, New York 14092
716-754-4883

International Travelers Hotline
Centers for Disease Control and Prevention
404-332-4559

Travel Medical, Inc.
351 Pleasant Street, Suite 312
Northampton, Massachusetts 01060
800-872-8633
If you're traveling to someplace exotic, send for a free catalog of special medical supplies.

INDEX

Accommodations. *See also* Lodgings
  at resorts and on cruises, 113
  on trains, 54–55
Acting games, 147–48
Active games, 144–53
Activities for children, 25
  at resorts and on cruises, 110–11, 114

Adapters for electrical appliances, 68–69
Adults
  activities for, 111–12
  meeting needs of, 5, 83, 96, 98
Advance preparations, 36–39
Adventure, as travel goal, 21
Ages of children
  impact on travel of, 10–17
  train travel and, 56, 58
Airports, 45, 47
Air pressure changes, 47, 73–74, 77
Air travel, 43–52
  air pressure changes during, 47, 73–74, 77
  amenities during, 46–47, 77
  baggage for, 70, 71
  charters and tours, 51–52
  choices in, 44–45
  fares for, 47–51
  infants and, 46–47, 48
  jet lag, 130–31
  managing children during, 76–79
  meals during, 46
  movies during, 47, 77–78
  reservations for, 50–51
  seats in, 45, 51
American Society of Travel Agents (ASTA), 29, 164
Amtrak, 53–56
Apartment rental. *See* Renting a home
Automobile associations and clubs, 28, 157

Babies. *See* Infants
Babysitting services, 5, 99
  in hotels, 86, 90
  in resorts and on cruises, 112
Baggage. *See also* Luggage
  for air travel, 70, 71

  insurance for, 34
  for train travel, 54
Ball games, 150–52
Balloon Toss (game), 148
Bed-and-breakfasts, 92–94, 159–60
Bedwetting, 67, 97
Book Race (game), 148
Books, travel, 7, 17, 27–28, 32, 84, 93, 120
Bookstores, travel, 162–63
Boredom, preventing, 9, 75–76, 78
Budget motels, 85–86, 161
Bulkhead seats, 45

Camping, 101–5, 118, 159
Card games, 141–43
Car rental, 58–61, 580
Car seats, 61, 67
Car sickness, 30–31
Car travel, 58–61, 81–83, 120–21. *See also* Recreational vehicles
  managing children during, 79–83
  single parents and, 120, 121
Categories (game), 137–38
Centers for Disease Control and Prevention (CDC), 125, 127
Chain hotels and motels, 85–86
Charades (game), 148
Charters. *See* Package tours
Children
  abilities of, 4, 10–17, 30
  airline meals for, 46
  fares for, 49–51, 55
  involving, in planning, 33, 73, 119–20
  rates for, hotel and motel, 86
Clapping Game, 137
Clothing, 65–66, 73
Coloring, 140
Connect the Dots (game), 140
Connecting flights, 44–45
Constipation, 130
Consulates, 34, 165–66
Converters for electrical appliances, 68–69
Costs, 5
  air travel, 44
  car rental, 59–60

Costs (*continued*)
  hotel and motel, 88–89
  recreational vehicle, 62, 63
  resort and cruise, 113–14
Cottage rental. *See* Renting a home
Counting games, 137
Courtesy, 107
Crazy Eights (game), 143
Cribs and cots, 11, 67, 86, 94
Cruises, 109–14, 160

Day pack, 71
Department of State Travel Advisory, 165
Departure, preparations for, 39–42, 72–73
Designated checker, 78, 107–8
Designing a trip, 31–39
Diarrhea, 130
Diary, trip, 81
Direct flights, 44
Discipline, 13
Discount fares
  for air travel, 48–51
  for train travel, 52–53, 55–56
Documents for travel, 33–35, 125, 164–65
Don't Say It (game), 139
Drinks, for travel, 74
Dude ranches, 113, 160
Duty-free allowance, 5

Educational aspects of travel, 6–8, 20–21
Electrical appliances abroad, 68–69
Embassies, 34, 165–66
Entertainment
  as travel goal, 20
  calendars, 32
Escape, as travel goal, 21

Family togetherness, as travel goal, 21–22, 116–17
Family travel
  apprehensions about, 4–6, 117–18
  benefits of, 6–9, 116–17
  limitations of, 3
Fares
  plane, 47–51
  train, 55–56, 57
Farm vacations, 93
Find the Letters (game), 137
Find the Most (game), 137
Find the Words (game), 141
First-aid kit, 132–34
Flinch (game), 151
Follow the Leader (game), 147

Food. *See also* Meals; Snacks
  air travel and, 78
  foreign, 32
  health risks and, 93, 123, 128
  during visits to friends and relatives, 106–7
Foreign Entry Requirements, 34
Foreign travel
  camping during, 102–3, 159
  car rental for, 59, 60, 160
  currency for, 38
  documents for, 33–35, 125, 164–65
  driving and, 34
  duty-free allowance, 5
  electrical appliances and, 68–69
  food shopping during, 98
  immunizations for, 34, 124–25
  information sources on, 27–29, 32, 160–67
  lodgings during, 87, 92–93, 94
  medical concerns about, 125–26, 127
  recreational vehicles for, 63–64
  by train, 56–58, 79, 159
Friends and relatives
  travel recommendations of, 26–27
  visiting, 22, 105–7, 119

Games, 135–52
Geography (game), 138
Global Emergency Medical Services, 127
Go Fish (game), 143
Grandparents, on family trips, 112
Guessing games, 136–37
Guess My Rhyme (game), 137
Guesthouses, 92–94
Guidebooks, 27–28, 32, 84, 93, 120, 162

Hangman (game), 140–41
Health concerns, 47, 123–34
Heat exhaustion, 131–32
Hit the Coin (game), 150
Hotels and motels, 85–92
  amenities in, 37, 90
  budget, 85–86, 161
  ratings for, 88
  special accommodations in, 87–88
  types of, 85–88
House rental. *See* Renting a house
House sitters, 36, 39

I Am Thinking of Something (game), 136
Imagination games, 139–40
I'm Going on a Trip (game), 140
Immunizations, 34, 124–25

Index • 169

Infants
  air travel and, 46–47, 48
  clothing for, 73
  needs and abilities of, 10–11
  packing for, 66–67, 73
  passports for, 33
Inns, 92–94
In the Soup (game), 150
Insurance
  car rental, 60
  health, 126
  homeowner's, 34
  medical, 34–35
  recreational vehicle rental, 63
  travel, 35
International Association for Medical Assistance to Travelers (IAMAT), 127
International Certificates of Vaccinations, 125
International driver's permit, 34
International Travelers Hotline, 125, 166
Itineraries, 34–35, 39

Jacks (game), 148–49
Jet lag, 130–31
Jump Rope (game), 148

Kickball (game), 151–52
Kick Relay (game), 150

Languages, 7–8
Limited movement games, 143–44
Lodgings, 84–108, 122
  in bed-and-breakfasts, 92–94
  in campgrounds, 102
  in guesthouses, 92–94
  in hotels and motels, 85–92
  in inns, 92–94
  last-minute, 94–95
  managing in, 95–99
  reservations for, 37, 119
  in resorts, 87, 109–14, 160–61
Lost articles, 78
Luggage, 69–71, 120. *See also* Baggage

Make Something Out of This (game), 140
Maps, 32, 85
May I (game), 145–46
Meals, 122
  during air travel, 46
  when camping, 103–4
  in hotels, 89
  in a recreational vehicle, 61

  in resorts and on cruises, 112–13, 114
  on the road, 82, 121
  on trains, 54, 79
Medical insurance, 34–35
Medical organizations, 126–27, 166
Medical records, 126
Medications, 47, 74–75, 124, 132–34
Memory games, 140
Middle childhood, travel and, 14–16
Milk, 93, 123, 128
Mirror Imitations (game), 147
Money
  children and, 15
  foreign, 38
  saving, 48–51, 91–92, 100, 121–23
  and single-parent travel, 121–23
  travelers' checks, 38
Motels. *See* Hotels and motels
Motion sickness, 129–30
Multiple Relay (game), 149–50
Museums, 4–5, 12, 21, 104

Nails for Sale (game), 144–45
Naps, 11, 14, 78, 79, 80, 82
National parks, 102, 159
National Train Timetables, 53, 54
Nonstop flights, 44

Old Maid (game), 142
Overbooking, in hotels and motels, 91

Package tours, 51–53, 56, 58
Packing, 39, 65–71, 72–73
  for camping, 104
  first-aid kit, 132–34
Passports, 33, 79, 164–65
Pencil and paper games, 140–41
Pests, 131
Physical invigoration, as travel goal, 19–20
Planning, 2–3, 18–42
  checklist for, 40–41
  children's involvement in, 33, 73, 119–20
  health-care, 124–27, 166
  as a single parent, 116, 118–20
  for train travel, 53–56
Post-trip boredom, 9
Pre-schoolers, needs and abilities of, 13–14

Rail passes, 57
Recreational vehicles (RVs), 61–64
  amenities in, 62–63
  managing children in, 80
  renting, 62, 63–64, 158

Red Light, Green Light (game), 146
Relay races, 149–50
Renting a home, 99–101, 103–5, 161–62
Reservations, 31, 37, 52, 119
    for air travel, 50–51
    for car rentals, 60
    for hotels and motels, 90–91
    for train travel, 54, 55
Resorts, 87, 109–14, 160–61
Rest and relaxation, as travel goal, 19
Rhythm games, 137–38
Rock, Scissors, Paper (game), 143–44
Running Bases (game), 150–51

Sausages (game), 138
Seat belts, 61
Shopping, for a trip, 37
Sidewalk Tennis (game), 151
Simon Says (game), 147
Single parents, 115–23
Sleeping, 54–55, 96–97, 129
Snacks, 73–74
    for air travel, 46
    in lodgings, 98
    for train travel, 79
Souvenirs, 15
Spiritual invigoration, as travel goal, 20
Stamina, developing, 20
Statues (game), 146
Storytelling (game), 139–40
Strollers, 11, 13, 67
Sunburn, 131–32
Swapping homes, 99–101, 103–5, 161–62
Swimming, 37, 82, 129

Tag (game), 149
Take a Trip Across the Country (game), 145
Tape players and tapes, 80–81
Teenagers
    needs and abilities of, 16–17
    physical challenges and, 20
    resorts and cruises and, 114
Telephone (game), 139

Tent camping, 101. *See also* Camping
Tips, 153–56
    camping, 104–5
    packing, 68, 69
Toddlers, needs and abilities of, 11–13
Toileting, 13, 42, 104
Tourist offices, 28, 32, 84–85, 93
Tour packages, 51–53, 56, 58
Toys, 75–76
    for car travel, 79–81
Train travel, 52–58
    baggage checking for, 54
    fares for, 55–56, 57
    food service during, 54
    foreign, 56–58, 79, 159
    information sources on, 158–59
    managing children during, 79
    sleeping accommodations during, 54–55
    within the U.S., 53–54
Transportation, 43–64
Travel agents, 29–30, 34, 110
    air travel and, 44
    lodgings and, 85
    organization of, 29, 164
Travel Bingo (game), 81
Travelers' checks, 38
Travel guides, 27–28, 32, 84, 93, 120, 162–63
Trip diary, 81
24 World Climate Charts, 127
20 Questions (game), 136

U.S. Public Health Service, 34

Vacation types, choosing, 22–29
Visas, 33–34

War (game), 141–42
Water, health risks and, 128
What Am I? (game), 147–48
What Could It Be (game), 139
Willy (game), 138–39
Word Change (game), 141
Word games, 138–39